Ojibwe

IN MINNESOTA

Anton Steven Treuer

 MINNESOTA HISTORICAL SOCIETY PRESS

Front cover: Josh DePerry dances at a Grand Portage powwow, 2009. Photo by Layne Kennedy
Back cover: Boys at Mille Lacs, ca. 1930. Photo by Monroe Killy, Minnesota Historical Society collections

Publication of this book was supported, in part, with funds provided by the Harriet Thwing Holden Fund for American Indian History.

www.mhspress.org

The Minnesota Historical Society Press is a member of the Association of American University Presses.

Manufactured in the United States of America.

10 9 8 7 6 5 4 3 2 1

♾ The paper used in this publication meets the minimum requirements of the American National Standard for Information Sciences—Permanence for Printed Library Materials, ANSI Z39.48–1984.

International Standard Book Number
ISBN 13: 978-0-87351-768-3 (paper)

Library of Congress Cataloging-in-Publication Data

Treuer, Anton Steven.
    Ojibwe in Minnesota / Anton Steven Treuer.
        p.   cm. — (The people of Minnesota)
    Includes bibliographical references and index.
    ISBN 978-0-87351-768-3 (pbk. : alk. paper) — ISBN 978-0-87351-795-9 (e-book)
        1. Ojibwa Indians—Minnesota—History. 2. Ojibwa Indians—Minnesota—Social life and customs. 3. Ojibwa Indians—Minnesota—Social conditions. I. Title.
E99.C6T74 2010
977.004'97333—dc22
                                                                                        2009047497

Cover design by Running Rhino Design.
Book design and composition by Wendy Holdman.
Printed by Sheridan Books, Ann Arbor, Michigan.

For my mother, Margaret Treuer, who taught me everything
I know about being Ojibwe in Minnesota

Contents

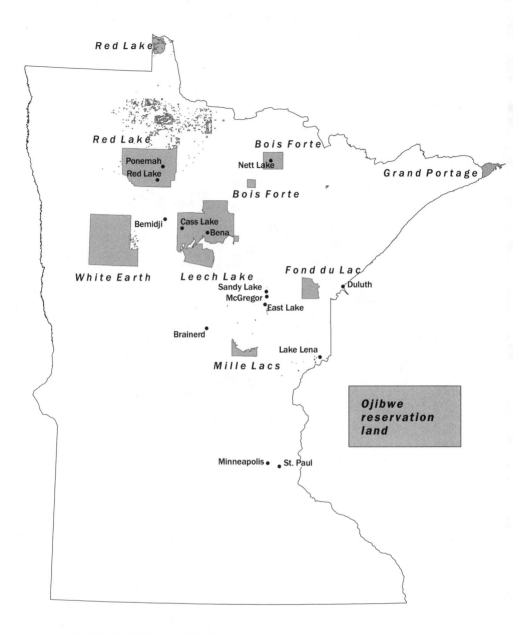

RESERVATION LOCATIONS AND POPULATIONS

Grand Portage (Cook County)	1,127
Mille Lacs (Mille Lacs, Aitkin, Crow Wing, Pine counties)	3,942
Leech Lake (Beltrami, Cass, Hubbard, Itasca counties)	8,861
Fond du Lac (Carleton, St. Louis counties)	4,044
White Earth (Mahnomen, Becker, Clearwater counties)	19,291
Bois Forte (Koochiching, Lake, Itasca, Cook counties)	3,052
Red Lake (Beltrami, Clearwater counties)	10,000

Ojibwe

IN MINNESOTA

Pipestone Singers at the Leech Lake Contest Powwow, September 6, 2009. Seated, from left to right, are George "Budman" Nayquonabe, Michael DeMain, Ahsinees Larson, Michael Sullivan, John Nayquonabe, Hunter Blassingane, and Wendall Powless.

P IPESTONE DRUM GROUP is singing at the Cass Lake powwow. High, powerful melody fills the air. Drumsticks pound in unison, igniting the rhythm of the dancers. Throngs of native and nonnative spectators surround the singers, recording the song on mp3 players, wav file recorders, and digital camcorders. It is powwow time again on the Leech Lake Indian Reservation in northern Minnesota, and Ojibwe culture is in motion.

The Pipestone Singers have made conscious choices to tenaciously hold onto older Ojibwe traditions. They all have Indian names and proudly represent their traditional Ojibwe clans—eagle, bear, and lynx. They come from different reservations, or off-reservation, in Minneapolis or other urban areas. Plenty of French, German, and Irish blood runs through their veins too. But they sing as one, and their singing is 100 percent Indian in style and tradition.

Pipestone is a little different from many drum groups in that most of their singers are members of the Midewiwin, the primary traditional religious society of the Ojibwe. Other drum groups have singers who are members of the Native American Church, a pan-Indian religious institution that combines traditional southwestern Indian use of peyote with Christianity. Many more are Christians of various denominations. And some feel they don't belong to any religion. Pipestone is also different in that most of their singers are members of Ojibwe Big Drums, which comprise one of the central ceremonial societies of the Ojibwe. They all attend ceremonies as instrumental parts of a resurging interest in traditional drum culture throughout Ojibwe country. The lead singer, Michael Sullivan, is pursuing a PhD in linguistics at the University of Minnesota and is part of a small but growing cadre of young leaders who seek to preserve and revitalize the Ojibwe language. They all have relatives in prison and relatives struggling with addiction to illegal drugs and alcohol. But they themselves were all at the Leech Lake powwow in September 2009—sober, healthy, and passionately involved in their culture.

Pipestone represents the future of the people as well as cultural continuity. But Pipestone also represents cultural change. They have consciously embraced modern education, clothes, music, and movies while trying to hold onto older Ojibwe traditions. Many drum members struggle to find the time to harvest wild rice or make maple sugar, as Ojibwe have for centuries. Few of them trap or play moccasin games, and none of them make birch-bark canoes as their ancestors did. They are busy going to powwows, working, attending school, and raising children. When they aren't listening to powwow music, they are listening to Fifty Cent, Ice Cube, and Eminem. They all have iPods and cell phones, loaded half and half with powwow music and hip-hop. They speak to one another in English, with a few Ojibwe words thrown in.

Powwow *Powwow* itself is new. It did not exist seventy years ago. It is a pan-Indian combination of Omaha grass dance ceremonies, Dakota war dances, Ojibwe dreams about the jingle dress, and rodeo customs, where dancers who used to parade into army forts in tribal war regalia now parade into the powwow arena in dance regalia for grand entry. There are many types of powwows. But the contest powwow at Leech Lake and others like it involve singers and dancers competing for money. Participants' abilities to sing and dance are highly valued, supplanting older cultural ideals of community cohesion, inclusiveness, and respectful generosity. The modern powwow is a welcome, healthy gathering of people from many communities. It is a joyous social event and source of community pride. But it is not a substitution for traditional Ojibwe religion or ways of life.[1]

Powwow is the largest and fastest-growing part of Ojibwe culture today. It is everywhere. Leech Lake spends over a hundred thousand dollars on prize money for its Labor

Day contest powwow alone; and Leech Lake has at least a dozen powwows a year, ranging in size from its large contest powwow to several smaller community powwows. The powwow budget for Leech Lake completely eclipses tribal expenditures on traditional culture and Ojibwe language revitalization. Tribes and tribal people are agents of their own cultural change.

Cultural change is constant for all people. French people are French even though they don't live in castles or wear armor while riding horses. They are still French even if they don't wear berets and smoke little pipes. Being French is something that is carried on the inside—in language, culture, and connection to place. And what it means to be French has changed over time. It is the same for the Ojibwe, whose music, political structure, economy, lifeways, and clan system have changed and evolved over time, in part because of negative experiences with Europeans, in part because of benign cultural exchange, but primarily by their own choices (some good, some bad).

The young men of the Pipestone drum are the future leaders of the Ojibwe in ceremony, education, and politics. They are working to preserve ceremonial drum culture and ancient Ojibwe tradition. And they are facilitating cultural change—inspiring and working for the proliferation of powwow culture and the educational, technological, economic, and political transformation of their people. They are a perfect cross-section of the paradoxically conflicting, yet also complementary, forces of cultural continuity and change that define exactly what it means to be Ojibwe in Minnesota.

Native Origins in the Americas

Many American history books assert that Indians became the first Native Americans when they arrived in this hemisphere nine to ten thousand years ago by crossing a frozen ice bridge that linked Asia to the Americas. Those books point to an archaeological site in Clovis, New Mexico, that contains human-made tools used to kill large mammals as the oldest indisputable evidence of humans in the hemisphere. What those books imply is that "we are all immigrants here." That implication, no matter how inadvertent, has sometimes been used to defend or justify the dispossession and genocide of this land's first inhabitants.

The widely held theory of human origin in the Americas (usually called the Bering Strait Theory or Clovis First Theory) is just a theory, not a fact, and there are obvious problems with it. If humans came from Asia to the Americas following herds of large vegetarian mammals ten thousand years ago, what did those large vegetarian mammals eat while walking across thousands of miles of ice? Or, if there was two-way traffic on the ice bridge, as is usually postulated (prehistoric horses and camels from the Americas to Asia at the same time that mammoths were going from Asia to the Americas), why would people follow food in one direction when other food was walking past them in the opposite direction?

But the greatest challenges to the Bering Strait Theory are scientific. Recent research on the Clovis site by Michael Water, Thomas Stafford, and others has confirmed human evidence there between 10,900 and 11,050 years ago. At Monte Verde in Chile, Mario Pino and Thomas Dillehay found human tool marks on mastodon bones and evidence of human-made structures dating back to 13,800 to 14,800 years ago. At the Meadowcroft Rockshelter in Pennsylvania, James M. Adovasio and other archaeologists have found tools, ceramics, lamellar blades, and lanceolate projectiles that are radiocarbon-dated sixteen to nineteen thousand years old. Those dates push evidence of human beings in the Americas back prior to when the last ice bridge connected the continents. At least fifty other major archaeological sites also suggest evidence of human existence in the Americas anywhere from nineteen to fifty thousand years ago. Archaeologists are still arguing about the dates and the validity of many sites, but increasingly the scientific community is saying that the Clovis First or Bering Strait model of human migration to the Americas is simply wrong.[i]

Archaeologists have not been able to determine when or how people first arrived in the Americas, although many new theories have been proposed in recent years. But we do know that people were here since before the last ice bridge seventeen to nineteen thousand years ago and probably much earlier. It is also important to note that when it comes to ancient civilizations (Egypt, Phoenicia, Greece, China), the earliest records we have are typically four to five thousand years old. There weren't even human beings anywhere in the British Isles twelve thousand years ago (the entire area was covered with ice). But there were Indians in the Americas then. No matter how one interprets the data, Native Americans are not immigrants. They are indigenous to the Americas.

Ojibwe Origins and Migration to Minnesota

Cultures and languages change far faster than most people realize. If you've ever tried to read Geoffrey Chaucer's *Canterbury Tales,* you realize that the English language as it was written six hundred years ago is barely discernible to a literate English speaker today. Ojibwe culture, language, and homeland have also undergone rapid transformation. Only three to four thousand years ago there were no people who called themselves *Ojibwe.* The ancestors of the Ojibwe were not living in what is now Minnesota but could be found throughout the northeastern part of North America and along the Atlantic Coast.[2]

Sometimes referred to by historians and linguists as Algonquian or Algic, this indigenous people eventually spread out and diversified throughout the continent. Today, twenty-seven different tribes trace their origins to this mother group. All of those tribes still share some common features of language and culture, but just as the differences between Romanian and French are significant within the Romance language family, so too are the differences between Ojibwe and Blackfeet, for example, within the Algonquian language family. The Ojibwe, Cree, Ottawa, and Potawatomi have long shared an intertwined economic and political history, and even today those languages remain very similar (as close as Spanish is to Portuguese). Other groups in the Algonquian language family such as the Cheyenne are so divergent from Ojibwe that a fluent speaker of one language can barely recognize a root word in the other.

The emergence of the Ojibwe as a distinct subgroup is hard to pinpoint but most likely happened around fifteen hundred years ago. Even then, the Ojibwe never functioned as one nation politically, economically, or even militarily but rather as a group of autonomous villages with many language and culture commonalities. Although there are many theories about the exact deeper meaning of the word

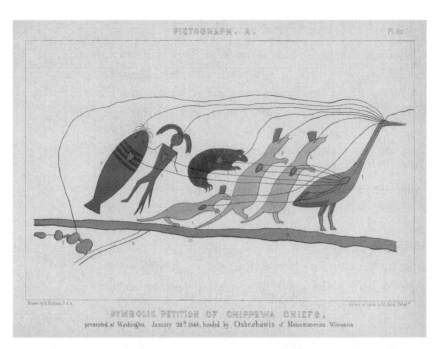

SYMBOLIC PETITION OF CHIPPEWA CHIEFS,
presented at Washington, January 28th 1849, headed by Oshcabawis of Monomonecau, Wisconsin

Chief Buffalo carried a birch-bark version of this image to Washington, DC, in 1849 to demonstrate the authority possessed by the chief delegation. The lines connecting the bullhead, merman, and martin clans to the crane are meant to show that the chiefs are in mental and spiritual agreement with one another and with the crane (Chief Buffalo) as their spokesman.

orgin of word Ojibwe

Ojibwe, it most likely comes from either the puckered seam of the Ojibwe moccasin or the Ojibwe custom of writing on birch bark.[3]

One key feature of Ojibwe culture was a very strong, deeply ingrained clan system. The English word *totem* is derived from the Ojibwe word for clan, *doodem.* Ojibwe clans were patrilineal, passed on through the father. When the Ojibwe first emerged as a distinct group, clan was probably the single most important factor in determining a

clan

person's place in society. Clan determined what kind of positions a person would be groomed for—politics, medicine, or military, for example. Marrying someone of the same clan, even if that person was not a blood relative, was strictly taboo in Ojibwe culture and the only wrongdoing that was considered a capital offense.[4]

Originally, all Ojibwe civil chiefs were of the loon or crane clans. However, as the Ojibwe moved west in the eighteenth century, warrior clans (bear, martin, lynx, and wolf) began to dominate. In what would later become Minnesota, entire villages were settled with no representation at all from traditional chieftainship clans. But those villages did have chiefs. They were simply elected from the local clans. At Red Lake in northern Minnesota, for example, the tribal flag today carries an image of the original clans that settled there—bear, turtle, bullhead, otter, eagle, martin,

flag → symbols of original tribes

Red Lake veterans John Barrett and Robert Desjarlait holding the Red Lake Nation Flag, Ponemah Traditional Powwow, 2009

and kingfisher—but no loon or crane. Although it has often been claimed that contact with Europeans changed and devalued the importance of clan for the Ojibwe, it was in fact the Ojibwe themselves who began to challenge and change traditional clan and leadership structure, long before Europeans arrived.[5]

The Ojibwe primarily lived in dome-shaped, bark-covered wigwams. The abundance of tamarack, maple, cedar, basswood, and birch throughout Minnesota made this type of dwelling the most practical to construct and keep warm. The Ojibwe also made several other types of lodges for ceremonies, maple sugar harvest, and travel.

Ojibwe culture revolved around the concept of reciprocity. Tobacco, food, and other gifts were offered with any harvest of plants or animals from the natural world for food, lodges, clothing, or medicine. There was a ceremony for every stage of life from birth to death, with great emphasis

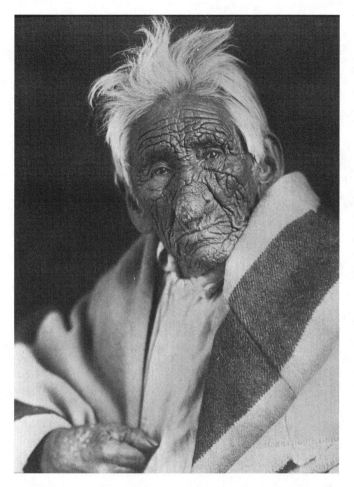

Age was highly respected in Ojibwe culture. The Ojibwe word for elder, *gichi-aya'aa*, literally means "great being." Pictured here is Leech Lake Ojibwe elder John Smith, one of the longest-lived people in history. He passed away at 137 years of age, having lived in three centuries. He was 131 when this picture was taken in 1915.

placed on puberty rituals and rights of passage that included fasting and vision quests for boys and sequestered instruction for girls. Age was highly venerated in Ojibwe culture. Ojibwe theology was based on a single creator but included a pantheon of other spirits as well, some of which had specific roles in life, such as Mishi-bizhiw, the underwater lion, who was the head of all water spirits and received special prayers for protection when ricing or fishing.[6]

The Ojibwe sustained their families by staying closely connected to the water. They fished more than they hunted. Fish
They hunted small game like rabbits, ducks, and geese even

Indians Gathering Wild Rice, Northern Minn.

J. P. OMICH BEMIDJI MINN.

HARVESTING WILD RICE.

Wild rice harvest near Bemidji, ca. 1905

more than big game (woodland caribou, elk, moose, and deer). While they farmed corn, beans, squash, and tobacco, they relied even more on harvesting berries, maple sugar, tubers, mushrooms, and especially wild rice that grows in lakes. Wild rice became so critical to the Ojibwe diet that it occupied a central place in the spiritual lore and customs of the people. There is a prophecy among the Ojibwe that they had to move west to "the land where food grows on water." This clear reference to wild rice was one of the major incentives that brought the Ojibwe from their ancestral homes on the Atlantic Coast to Minnesota.[7]

The natural food resources on the Atlantic Coast were so tremendous that they sustained a large and dense population (greater than that of Western Europe). However, around the time that the Ojibwe emerged as a distinct people within the Algonquian language family, that population density created powerful competition between tribes over territory and resources on the land. In part because

Wild rice harvest on Lake Number Four, near Walker, 1939

of tribal warfare and in part because of the prophecies, the Ojibwe slowly began to migrate westward around fifteen hundred years ago. Other tribes already occupied all of North America at this time. How strongly other tribes contested Ojibwe migration is not well known. Ojibwe oral history suggests, and the archaeological record confirms, that the Ojibwe moved slowly in small groups over a period of hundreds of years primarily through the St. Lawrence Seaway and the central Great Lakes. By the time the French arrived in the Great Lakes at the beginning of the seventeenth century, the Ojibwe were already well established at Sault Ste. Marie and the surrounding area and no longer had ties to their old village sites on the Atlantic Coast.[8]

The Ojibwe Fur-trade Era, 1640–1820

When James Fenimore Cooper wrote *The Last of the Mohicans,* he did a lot more than write a popular white love story

Hunting on snowshoes, ca. 1870

Lact of the

with an Indian background. He created a common adage for American understandings of Indian history: "the last of the _____," where the blank is the name of every tribe in the Americas. Later codified in the term *Manifest Destiny*, this was the idea that when the white man showed up, the Indian began to decline and fade away, leaving the continent to the unchallenged ascension of European Americans. Most people understand the fur trade as just the opening push toward this inevitable conclusion.

The Ojibwe have a very different understanding of their history. It took the French forty years from their arrival in the St. Lawrence around 1600 to reach the Ojibwe people concentrated around Sault Ste. Marie, and then with only a couple of Jesuit priests. Over the next hundred years, the French expanded their domain and economic empire in North America through the good graces and political, military, and economic might of the Ojibwe. Through their interactions with the French during the fur-trade era, the Ojibwe increased their standard of living, grew in population (which had been devastated by terrible disease pandemics), expanded their political power, and multiplied their territorial holdings by a factor of twenty. By the time the French were finally evicted from North America by the British at the conclusion of the French and Indian War in 1760, the Ojibwe had expanded their territory from the central Great Lakes eastward into Michigan, Ontario, and Quebec and westward through Michigan's Upper Peninsula, Wisconsin, and Minnesota. Ojibwe expansion would continue westward for another century, at the expense of other native nations, into North Dakota, Montana, northern Ontario, Manitoba, and Saskatchewan. Whose destiny was manifest is entirely a matter of perspective.

Expansion

Interaction with French and British traders during the fur-trade era altered Ojibwe life forever. The Ojibwe obtained new technologies, such as metal tools, traps, beads, cloth, paint, and guns. In addition, although the Ojibwe had a trade and barter system in place before contact with Europeans, their economy transformed through the fur trade. More than ever before, people developed highly specialized skills such as trapping. They traded their furs for what they needed rather than harvesting and making all goods and foods themselves. Ojibwe relationships with the natural world changed as Indians harvested beavers to extinction in large areas, fueling more intense competition over the land with other tribes.[9]

The Ojibwe were at the center of the trade, and it was a powerful position. Their military and trade allegiance was actively courted by both the French and the British. Ojibwe trade was so critical to Europeans that French and British politicians, traders, and citizens adopted many Ojibwe protocols in dealing with all tribal peoples. Thus Europeans tended to favor Ojibwe customs—use of pipes, councils, cooperative diplomacy, and barter systems—when meeting

favor Ojibwe meeting customs

Anishinaabe and
French fur trader

with the Ojibwe and any other Indian peoples. The Ojibwe language became the lingua franca of the fur trade, and this helps to explain why Ojibwe names dominate maps of the Great Lakes even today, whether those maps were made by the French, the British, or the Americans. The French in particular sought to cement their relationships with the Ojibwe by arranging marriages between their fur brokers and Ojibwe women, blending the blood and cultures of both people. Even today, more than a third of Ojibwe band members in Minnesota carry French surnames.[10]

War and Change

The rising standard of living the Ojibwe enjoyed as a result of the fur trade came with a price. Competition between the French and the British was intense. Natural resources were abundant but finite. Both factors led to a bloodbath in the Great Lakes that nearly annihilated entire tribes and depopulated entire regions. Here, too, the Ojibwe were at the center of the story.

For sixty years, the Ojibwe were embroiled in conflict with their eastern neighbors over land and the resources obtained from the land. From 1641 to 1701, the Dutch and then the British armed and encouraged the Iroquois Confederacy (in the eastern Great Lakes) to attack the French in order to disrupt their trade. They also encouraged the Iroquois to attack various Indian tribes such as the Huron and Ojibwe in order to push them westward and obtain exclusive access to their trapping grounds. Initially, the French were reluctant to arm their Indian trading partners. But when the conflict became too costly for the French to ignore, they cemented their alliance with the Ojibwe, Ottawa, and Potawatomi, collectively known as the Three Fires Confederacy.[11]

The Ojibwe enjoyed many military advantages over the Iroquois because of geography. Ojibwe families, for example, were more isolated from conflict zones than were Iroquois families. The more populous Ojibwe villages lay upstream

military advantages

Ojibwe and other French-allied Indians fighting the British at the Battle of Monongahela, July 9, 1755, during the French and Indian War

and in strategic locations. The Ojibwe also maintained an advantage in their larger but lighter and faster birch-bark canoes. The Iroquois and Dakota both used wooden canoes fashioned from dug-out logs. Over time, the Ojibwe and their allies pushed the Iroquois back from the central Great Lakes into New York and absorbed the largely depopulated Huron territory between them. Eventually, the Three Fires Confederacy occupied much of southern Ontario, Quebec, and the surrounding region. The Iroquois were crushed by 1701, and the British were tired of the physical and economic cost of the conflict. The British and French made peace and drew lines between their territorial claims in the Treaty of Utrecht in 1713. Territorial conflict between the Ojibwe and their eastern neighbors was finally over.

French-British trade rivalry continued, and outright conflict between the European powers renewed with even greater vigor during the Seven Years' War (1756–63) and its North American theater of conflict, often referred to as the French and Indian War (1754–60). The French were ultimately evicted from the region in 1760. An Ottawa chief named Pontiac led a pan-Indian alliance—including many Ojibwe—against the British in 1763. Called Pontiac's War, this conflict brought nine of the eleven British forts in the Great Lakes under Indian control. But because Pontiac never gained the support and intervention promised by the French, his efforts changed little in the new dynamic between the British and the Indians. The Ojibwe participated in the French and Indian War, Pontiac's War, Tecumseh's conflict (1810–13), and the War of 1812 (1812–15). During the War of 1812, Wisconsin Ojibwe chief Mangizid (Big Foot) was actually commissioned as a general in the British army. At the same time, a group of Grand Portage Ojibwe received British medals for service to the crown. But all of those conflicts embroiled the eastern Ojibwe far more than their western brothers. The Minnesota Ojibwe participated in significant, but not overwhelming, numbers. The most

French & British
peace &
draw lines

War
History

important long-term developments of the fur-trade period for the Minnesota Ojibwe were French-Ojibwe intermarriages, the eastward expansion of their territory, and their emergence as the dominant tribal military and economic power in the Great Lakes.[12]

Ojibwe-Dakota Relations

During the fur-trade era and into the 1800s, Ojibwe relations with the neighboring Dakota were far more important than their relationships with the French, British, or Americans. Although historians tend to emphasize conflict between the two tribes, there was more peace than war between the Ojibwe and Dakota. The economic, social, and cultural exchanges between them were truly formative for both groups.

In the mid-1600s, Ojibwe conflict with the Iroquois in the eastern Great Lakes was so brutal that many Ojibwe people sought refuge from the warfare with their Dakota neighbors to the west. In 1659, Father Allouez, a Jesuit priest, observed that more than four thousand Ojibwe people, and other tribes, had settled at Chequamegon Bay, Wisconsin, near present-day Duluth, Minnesota, in what was usually considered Dakota territory. The Dakota welcomed the Ojibwe and other tribal refugees at first because they saw potential trade gains. The Dakota approached their visitors and, according to Nicolas Perrot, "began, according to their custom, to weep over every person they met, in order to manifest the lively joy they felt in meeting them; and they entreated the strangers to have pity on them ... [thanking the Great Spirit] for having guided to their country these peoples. [The Dakota] loaded them with endearing terms and showed the utmost submissiveness, in order to touch them with compassion." The Ojibwe behaved similarly.[13]

In 1679, as the Ojibwe gained the upper hand in their eastern conflict with the Iroquois, they also cemented a strong diplomatic relationship with the Dakota. The two tribes needed things from each other. The Ojibwe were the linchpin to French defense and supply of the fur trade and were kept well outfitted in muskets, kettles, and other European trade goods as a result. The Ojibwe were powerful and numerous, with a population around sixty thousand in spite of warfare and disease epidemics. However, the Ojibwe lands around Sault Ste. Marie had been drastically overhunted and overtrapped. They needed new areas to hunt and trap in order to maintain their standard of living and meet French needs for furs. The Dakota held a huge territory with an abundance of furs, but they were too far away to actively and consistently engage the French in trade.[14]

Alliance, 1679–1736

The Ojibwe and the Dakota formed an alliance in 1679 at Fond du Lac at the outlet of the St. Louis River, in what would later be Minnesota. This was probably the largest diplomatic event among Indians in North America observed—but not orchestrated—by Europeans. French explorers Nicolas Perrot and Daniel Greysolon, Sieur du Lhut (later corrupted into *Duluth*), attended. Ultimately, the Dakota allowed the Ojibwe to hunt and settle on much of their territory east of the Mississippi River in Minnesota and Wisconsin. Through peaceful diplomacy, La Pointe, Chequamegon Bay, Keweenaw Bay, Lac Courte Oreilles, Lac du Flambeau, and Fond du Lac became Ojibwe possessions after 1679. In return, the Ojibwe kept the Dakota well supplied with guns, knives, kettles, and other trade goods and sold Dakota furs to the French. The Ojibwe assumed the lucrative role of middlemen in Dakota-French trade.

The peace agreement was mutually beneficial. Both the Dakota and the Ojibwe were better protected militarily. Both stood to gain economically. The French profited as well, dramatically expanding their markets and fur supplies

Daniel Greysolon, Sieur du Lhut, at the St. Louis River outlet. Spirit Mountain looms in the background.

DANIEL GREYSOLON SIEUR DULHUT
AT THE HEAD OF THE LAKES — 1679

without increasing their own labor or management costs. During the period of peace, the Dakota and the Ojibwe both grew in economic and political importance as well as population.

The Ojibwe-Dakota peace had immediate and long-lasting effects. As early as 1682, Ojibwe traders were traveling more than 150 miles into Dakota territory to pick up Dakota furs and deliver European trade goods. At the same time, more than a thousand Ojibwe had permanently settled at La Pointe on Madeline Island and many had spread out over the Chequamegon Bay area and deep into the interior of Wisconsin. The bounty of mainland Wisconsin and

Minnesota, where both the Ojibwe and the Dakota hunted, often together, was tremendous. There was an abundance of moose, caribou, buffalo, elk, and every kind of furbearing animal imaginable. The enduring peace between the Ojibwe and the Dakota brought heightened prosperity and cross-cultural exchange, as the Ojibwe shared their primary religious society, the Midewiwin or Medicine Dance, with the Dakota. The Wakan Dance, as the Dakota called it, proliferated and dominated Dakota religious experience in Minnesota. The Ojibwe-Dakota tribal entente endured for fifty-seven years.[15]

share dance [handwritten annotation in margin]

Ojibwe-Dakota Conflicts

The eruption of hostilities between the Ojibwe and Dakota people in 1736 is a long and complicated story. A full description is beyond the purview of this book, but a brief overview is essential. The trouble began when Pierre Gaultier de Varennes, Sieur de la Vérendrye, was commissioned by the government of New France to find the Northwest Passage to the Pacific. La Vérendrye's son, Jean Baptiste, was adopted by the Cree at the French post in Rainy Lake and accompanied a joint Cree-Assiniboine war expedition against the Dakota and their Nakota brothers at Red Lake, Minnesota. The Dakota and their Ojibwe allies retaliated, killing nineteen of the twenty-one Frenchmen in the Rainy

---

Ojibwe-Dakota Intermarriage

Some of the most influential Ojibwe and Dakota leaders were born of peacetime intermarriages. Dakota chiefs Wabasha and Red Wing and Ojibwe chiefs Big Foot, White Fisher, Flat Mouth, and many others were of mixed Ojibwe-Dakota heritage. The Ojibwe chief of Rice Lake, Wisconsin, and the Dakota chief of Yellow Lake, Wisconsin, were brothers, sharing a Dakota father. Even after hostilities erupted between the Dakota and the Ojibwe, these two brothers kept the peace between their respective communities for many years. In addition, the prominent wolf and kingfisher clans were introduced to the Ojibwe through Dakota paternity in mixed marriages.[iv]

Lake area, including La Vérendrye's son. La Vérendrye, in turn, abandoned his diplomatic and trade mission and expended all French resources to avenge his son's death. He armed the Cree and their allies for war against the Dakota, whom he held exclusively responsible—in spite of Ojibwe participation in his son's death. The Ojibwe had to choose between their alliance with the French, Ottawa, and Potawatomi and their entente with the Dakota.

The Ojibwe ultimately maintained their French and Three Fires allegiances, attacking the Dakota. The Cree and Assiniboine were supposed to coordinate attacks against the Dakota that year, but a devastating smallpox epidemic prohibited their participation en masse. As a result, the Dakota, who expected vengeance from the Cree, Assiniboine, and possibly the French, found themselves under assault only by their longtime friends, the Ojibwe. They swiftly and furiously counterattacked, forcing many Ojibwe from their homes in Minnesota and Wisconsin.

Intense territorial conflict between the Ojibwe and the Dakota dominated tribal life in Minnesota from 1736 to 1760. Few battles were witnessed and written about by European observers, so the historical record has been pieced together with oral accounts from both tribes, archaeological evidence, and secondhand European accounts. Major battles occurred at Sandy Lake (1744), Kathio-Mille Lacs (1745), Leech Lake (1760), and Red Lake (1770). In spite of the extraordinary danger involved, the Ojibwe immediately settled Dakota villages with their families after killing or routing all the former inhabitants. Sometimes, Dakota counterattacks wiped out the entire Ojibwe population at the newly settled villages, only to have the process repeated again the next year. Usually, battles were relatively brief, but at Kathio (near Mille Lacs), the Ojibwe and the Dakota battled for three days. The Ojibwe eventually charged the village in overwhelming numbers, dropping gunpowder wrapped in cloth through smoke holes in the Dakota lodges,

Ojibwe and Dakota Indians at the Battle of the Brule River, October 1842. Chief Buffalo engineered a double-envelopment of the Dakota forces, killing 101 enemy warriors and losing only thirteen of his own.

killing hundreds, and then clubbing hundreds more as they emerged from their dwellings, concussed and blinded by smoke from the explosions.[16]

Ojibwe-Dakota conflict was brutal. Men, women, and children were all considered equally honorable targets in warfare. Combat was primarily hand-to-hand, and casualty rates were exceptionally high. For many years, there was a stretch of no-man's-land between Ojibwe and Dakota villages that neither tribe dared occupy in the summer when warfare was at its height. But both groups exploited this area for hunting, fishing, and trapping in the winter as a necessary means of survival. It took several years from the onset of hostilities for Ojibwe advantages in trade technology, upstream village locations, the birch-bark canoe (swifter, lighter, and more buoyant than Dakota dugouts), and population concentrations on the Ojibwe-Dakota frontier to turn the tide of battle in their favor. By 1770, the Ojibwe had permanent and exclusive control over the northern half of Minnesota. Some areas in central Minnesota, including Brainerd, Crow Wing, and Gull Lake, were added to Ojibwe land holdings in the early 1800s.

Warfare between the Ojibwe and the Dakota in Minnesota persisted after 1770, but war expeditions greatly diminished in size from groups of twelve hundred warriors or more to groups of twenty or fewer, with only a few notable exceptions. Both the Ojibwe and the Dakota believed that the soul of a person killed in battle was offended and that offense inhibited their peaceful departure to the spirit world. The offense could be removed ceremonially or by avenging the death in a retaliatory strike. This deep cultural belief helps explain why warfare continued for decades even after territorial conflicts in Minnesota had long been resolved.

Both tribes abandoned intertribal conflict by the middle of the nineteenth century. There was a massive surge in white settlement at this time, and both tribes were overwhelmed with new challenges brought by the Americans. Furthermore, this was when the Dakota presented the first ceremonial Big Drum to the Ojibwe people as a peace offering. The ceremony that came with the drum became and still remains a dominant part of Ojibwe culture today. Relations between the Ojibwe and the Dakota throughout the continent continue to be peaceful and supportive in the modern era, as both tribes participate in each other's powwows and social, ceremonial, and political events.[17]

Ojibwe-Dakota Battles in Minnesota	
Sandy Lake	1744
Kathio-Mille Lacs	1745
St. Croix River	1755
Leech Lake	1760
Red Lake	1770

spirits of dead

Treaties and Reservations

Ojibwe lives changed dramatically between their migration from the Atlantic and their settlement of northern Minnesota. But the pace and nature of change accelerated

Ojibwe and Dakota dancing at White Earth, 1910

1819-1825

beyond anyone's imagining once Americans arrived in the region. From 1819 to 1825, the U.S. Army built the first white settlement in what would become the state of Minnesota. In spite of French and British trade in the region and an early American exploratory tour in 1805 by Zebulon Montgomery Pike up the Mississippi River and deep into Ojibwe country, the entire area was occupied and used exclusively by the Anishinaabe. However, after the construction of Fort Snelling at the confluence of the Mississippi and Minnesota rivers, the U.S. Army, government, and civilian presence in Minnesota grew rapidly. Minnesota became a territory in 1848 and a state in 1858.

The influx of nonnative people into Minnesota during the 1800s was devastating to the Ojibwe. Within the living memory of an Ojibwe person, the Anishinaabe went from being a regional power with sovereign control over large tracts of territory to being disempowered occupants

of a small portion of their original homelands. Challenges
came from many directions.

At the same time that American military personnel and
civilians were moving into Minnesota, the Ojibwe economy fell into chaos. There was a major glut in the fur market, followed by cycles of collapse and rebuilding. Demand
and prices for furs hit a bottom just as the U.S. government
made its first overtures for the acquisition of Ojibwe land.
In addition, the lucrative and powerful role of middleman
that the Ojibwe had enjoyed when trading with the French
and the British evaporated with the Americans, who
placed their own licensed traders throughout the continent.
Métis traders now dominated the trade. The Métis were of
mixed French and Ojibwe heritage but had their own language (Michif), culture, communities, and loyalties. They

Ojibwe Economy in chaos

Fort Snelling, with
native settlement
in the foreground,
1850

used overland oxcart trails more than rivers to bring furs to the market, circumventing Ojibwe villages. Ojibwe economic power was waning, and their standard of living was declining for the first time in their long history.

When the U.S. government initially asked the Ojibwe to sell land in Minnesota in 1837, the Ojibwe were willing to entertain any ideas that might buoy their economy. The Ojibwe insisted on what was important to them—access to the land for hunting, fishing, and trapping. The Treaty of 1837 included clauses that protected Ojibwe rights to use—for those purposes—all land they sold. Title to the land was an alien concept to the Ojibwe. Cash payment for title seemed a great deal as long as the Anishinaabe didn't lose the right to use the land. Ultimately, the land flooded

Treaty of 1837 [handwritten annotation]

Ojibwe and other Indians at the Treaty of Prairie du Chien, 1825, a "peace and friendship" agreement that drew lines between Ojibwe and Dakota lands in Minnesota but also set the stage for subsequent land cessions

with white settlers and both access to and use of the land were denied to the Ojibwe in spite of their treaty-protected rights. This legal discord would set the stage for an Ojibwe treaty rights case that went all the way to the U.S. Supreme Court in 1999.[18]

Land cession treaties introduced a vicious cycle. The Ojibwe economy depended on resources obtained from the land. As the land used by the Ojibwe declined in size, so too did their economy and standard of living. These factors created greater pressure on the Ojibwe to sell more land to produce more cash to feed families in increasingly dire straits. Ultimately, the short-term benefits of the treaties never compensated for the long-term loss of the land. Traditional lifeways were irrevocably altered, and poverty became a common experience for the Ojibwe.

debt cycle

The Minnesota State Seal, approved in 1861, shows the Indian leaving, riding west into the setting sun, and the white farmer industriously working the land, keeping a wary eye on the Indian.

Pressure mounted on the Anishinaabe throughout the nineteenth century. Finally, in 1850, President Zachary Taylor issued orders for the removal and relocation of the Ojibwe from Michigan, Wisconsin, and Minnesota to Sandy Lake in central Minnesota. Ojibwe from throughout the region who had signed treaties in good faith were told that they could only collect their payments at Sandy Lake, which for many was a great distance from their homes. When thousands of Ojibwe massed at Sandy Lake late into the fall, government agents and Minnesota Territorial Governor Alexander Ramsey refused to disburse payments. The food rations supplied to the Ojibwe by the Americas were meager, and some of them were spoiled. After eating those rations, the Ojibwe suffered an outbreak of dysentery and other diseases. Hundreds died from disease and exposure as they finally returned to their home communities in the harsh winter weather. Afterward, the U.S. government focused its

"Removal"

disease

Treaty Period Chronology

Fort Snelling constructed	1819-25
Ojibwe land cession treaties	1837, 1847, 1854, 1855, 1863, 1864, 1866, 1867
Minnesota becomes a territory	1848
Sandy Lake Annuity Fiasco	1850
Minnesota becomes a state	1858
Dawes Act (allotment)	1887
Nelson Act (Minnesota allotment and Red Lake land cession)	1889
Battle of Sugar Point	1898

removal pressure on relocating Ojibwe people to White Earth in northwestern Minnesota, where a large reservation was to be established.[19]

Reservations

The Sandy Lake Annuity Fiasco of 1850 did not succeed in permanently concentrating and relocating the Ojibwe people. But it did set the stage for a devastating series of land cession treaties from 1854 to 1867 that stripped most of Minnesota out of Ojibwe hands and settled most Ojibwe people on reservations. The Ojibwe did not want to give up their land or traditional lifeways, but they were forced to choose between accommodating the very unreasonable demands of the United States and engaging in outright war over the land. By the time the U.S. government wanted to create reservations for the Ojibwe, most Anishinaabe chiefs had already been to Fort Snelling and Washington, DC. They had seen the torrid growth of white settlement in Minnesota and the reach of the U.S. Army. The futility of war was obvious. Plus, with the fur trade in decline and disease and hunger in Ojibwe villages on the rise, reservations seemed to be the lesser of two evils. In 1854 and 1855, the Ojibwe sold millions of acres in Minnesota and accepted settlement on several reservations. Further land cessions followed, and in 1867 many Ojibwe were

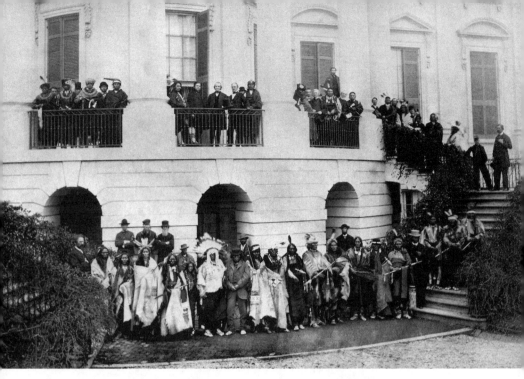

Indian delegation to Washington, DC, 1867. Chief Hole in the Day (Bagone-giizhig) of Crow Wing (on balcony, to the right of the second pillar from the left) represented Ojibwe interests in negotiating removal to White Earth.

pressured to abandon existing reservations and relocate to White Earth.

Reservations permanently changed and eroded the sovereign power of the Ojibwe people. Tribal chiefs were denied the right to govern their own people. Instead, the Ojibwe were governed by bureaucrats called Indian agents. These agents took over the power—previously held by chiefs—to decide who received treaty monies and where and when monies would be distributed. In place of traditional tribal councils, the U.S. government established Courts of Indian Offenses to handle all civil and criminal matters. While reservation police forces sometimes employed Indians, they could only enforce the edicts of the government-established courts and government-appointed agents. Tribal chiefs, councils, and Ojibwe concepts of

change govt

Indian
Reorganization
Act 1934

justice were ignored for nearly a century. After passage of the Indian Reorganization Act in 1934, tribes were allowed once again to organize their own governments, but by then Ojibwe ideas and institutions of justice, government, and leadership had been so thoroughly eroded that all of the reservations in Minnesota adopted democratic governing systems based loosely on American ideals and structures. Reservations assimilated Ojibwe politics just as thoroughly as they destroyed the Ojibwe economy.[20]

Government policies on reservations not only eroded the power of tribal leaders but also restricted the ability of the Ojibwe to practice their traditional religion. In 1882, the Bureau of Indian Affairs (BIA), the government agency that managed dealings with the tribes, created a List of Indian Offenses. Banned activities for tribal members included dances, giveaways, feasts, and religious gatherings. The BIA reinforced that list with directives to Indian agents on each reservation. One of those directives, called Circular 1665, instructed Indian agents to suppress tribal dances and ceremonies and remained in effect until 1933, within the living memory of many tribal members today. It is painfully ironic that the U.S. government was ostensibly created in large part to protect freedom of religion and incorporated that idea into the First Amendment to the Constitution but actively suppressed the religious freedom of the land's first inhabitants.[21]

While tribal members struggled to hold onto traditional religious practices in the late 1800s, Christian missionaries came to the reservations. Numerous denominations competed with one another for access to Ojibwe souls. Americans had no interest in allowing or empowering the Anishinaabe to make their own religious choices at the time. Some Ojibwe communities resisted. In Ponemah, on the Red Lake Reservation, the Catholic Church twice tried to build a church, mission, and school, only to have tribal members burn all buildings to the ground each time. To this day

Ponemah,
Red Lake
Reservation

there has never been a Christian funeral in the community, as all members steadfastly hold to traditional Ojibwe religious beliefs. The majority of Mille Lacs members also adhere to Ojibwe religion. Most other Minnesota Ojibwe reservations are over 50 percent Christian. White Earth is approximately 90 percent Christian, spread among various denominations.

Boarding Schools

Even before the formation of reservations, the U.S. government made clear that its goal was to assimilate Indians into the broader, white culture. Back in 1818, the first U.S. Congressional Committee on Indian Affairs met and proclaimed, "In the present state of our country, one of two things seems to be necessary; either that those sons of the forest should be moralized or exterminated." The residential boarding school system was an important component in "moralizing," or assimilating, Indians. It focused on native children and had a profound impact on Ojibwe families.[22]

Beginning in the late nineteenth century, missionary, military, and government officials advocated the removal of Indian children from their homes to better instruct them in the English language and American culture. Captain Richard Henry Pratt was superintendent of the Carlisle Indian Industrial School, the first of many boarding schools created for Indian children. "Our goal," Pratt stated, "is to kill the Indian in order to save the man." The idea of the schools had less to do with giving children an education than it did with taking away their culture. Children

After the assassination of Ojibwe chief Hole in the Day (Bagone-giizhig) of Crow Wing, in 1868, U.S. government control of White Earth and other reservations solidified. Trader Augustus Aspinwall wrote of the chief's death, "The government done nothing with the murderers . . . It was much easier for the agents to get along with these Indians after Hole-in-the-Day's death, as he was the smartest Indian chief the Chippewa Indians ever had."

Ojibwe and other Indian students at an unknown boarding school, ca. 1900

were sent to schools far from home in order to discourage running away and to inhibit parental contact. Their clothes were burned and their hair cut. They were strictly forbidden to speak tribal languages. At Carlisle and many other schools, children spent half the day working in fields or digging ditches and half the day in class.

Parents did have the option of sending their children to mission schools instead, but those schools were usually just as harsh in suppressing tribal languages and culture and even more likely to expose students to sexual molestation, which was commonly reported. Attendance at BIA boarding schools like Carlisle or church mission schools was compulsory for Indian children—homeschooling and public schools were not legal options for Indian youth in the late nineteenth century.

Parents often initially thought that their children would benefit from opportunities upon graduation. They knew their children would receive at least three meals a day at the schools, which was more than many families could provide. Yet the residential boarding schools in particular were devastating for most families. On returning home, many children no longer recognized their own parents and could not speak the same language. Promised economic opportunities for graduates never materialized. Children often felt they could not fit in either on or off the reservations, and those feelings, together with the dire poverty prevailing in most places, simply added to growing dysfunction on the reservations.

The long-term effects of the residential boarding school system were profound. People learn how to parent by how they are parented, but with as many as three generations of Ojibwe people going through BIA boarding schools, a critical piece of the social fabric was severely damaged. Many Ojibwe families have rebounded from the effects of boarding schools, but their blessings are derived in spite of the system rather than because of it.

Social aspect of tribe damaged

It took a long time for the boarding school policy to be reformed. The schools came under criticism after many children began to die from malnutrition and diseases like tuberculosis without their bodies even being sent home for burial. The commissioner of Indian Affairs defended these and other practices in 1899, saying, "This education policy is based on the well known inferiority of the great mass of Indians in religion, intelligence, morals, and home life." There were twenty-five such schools in operation that year, with twenty thousand new students every year. The schools came under increasing scrutiny and attack as more than half of the children at Carlisle had trachoma by 1900 and an influenza outbreak at Haskell in 1918 killed more than three hundred students. Official modifications did not change the dynamic, and Carlisle closed in 1918, but other schools actually continued to increase their enrollments. In 1928, the U.S. government commissioned the Merriam Report, which blasted the schools for poor nutrition and health care for students, insufficient clothing, exceedingly harsh physical punishment, and the breakup of tribal families. The next commissioner of Indian Affairs, John Collier, actively tried to dismantle and reform the BIA school system. It took many years, but after World War II, day schools

Education system condemned

started to dominate the educational experience of Ojibwe children in Minnesota. There are still a few BIA-operated boarding schools in existence today, but their policies have been thoroughly reformed.[23]

The day schools often did little to counteract the damage done by boarding schools. They still had strict English-only policies. Children were often suspended for having long hair. Native children still had to learn about the history, government, and economy of others and rarely, if ever, about themselves. Recent modifications to curriculum and tribal control of some schools have begun to turn the tide and enable Ojibwe children to learn about their own people in school, but it's just a beginning. There remains a tremendous disconnect in Ojibwe communities today about the value of formal education and the educational system's abilities to meet native needs. As a result, dropout rates for Ojibwe youth are nearly four times higher than they are for the general population and as much as twelve times higher in some areas.[24]

Both local day schools and distant residential boarding schools had a profound impact on native languages, including Ojibwe. Today, 190 of the remaining 210 tribal languages spoken in the United States are likely to go extinct in the next thirty years because only elders speak those languages. Ojibwe survives largely because of the strength of fluency in remote parts of Canada, but Ojibwe dialects on the U.S. side of the border are in grave jeopardy, as there are now fewer than a thousand Ojibwe speakers in the United States and most of them are elders.[25]

Struggles over Land

While the Ojibwe faced challenges to their culture and sovereignty, they also struggled to maintain control over their remaining land. The Ojibwe had been settled on reservations in Minnesota with the promise that they would retain

Don't learn Native history

Languages going extinct

Ojibwe girls at
Ponemah Indian
School, 1940

those lands in perpetuity. However, with the ink barely dry
on the first treaties, the U.S. government introduced new
treaties and executive orders shrinking the size and number of reservations. White Earth and Leech Lake each endured several congressional acts and executive orders that
reduced or altered the dimensions of their reservations.

treaties did not last long.

The U.S. government stopped making land cession treaties with the Ojibwe in 1871 but continued to erode tribal
lands through other means into the next century. At Leech
Lake, in northern Minnesota, the government created the
Chippewa National Forest in 1928, which includes 85 percent of the reservation. The Leech Lake Ojibwe were forced
to find homes for their people on the remaining 15 percent
of their lands. After the creation of the Chippewa National
Forest, the Ojibwe would never again have control of the
resources or land that make up the overwhelming majority of their reservation. Starting with Chippewa National
Forest and continuing today, the U.S. government has been
reluctant to allow the tribe to share management of the
natural resources on the reservation or any of the financial advantages. National forests are regularly logged and
the timber sold, of continued benefit to the U.S. government but to the economic and ecological detriment of the

still eroding Land from reservations

Ojibwe people living on the reservation. Similar acts created the Tamarac National Wildlife Refuge on the White Earth Reservation and the Rice Lake National Wildlife Refuge on the Mille Lacs Reservation, effectively denying Ojibwe access to huge portions of their own reservations without consent or compensation.[26]

Allotment

While land cession treaties, government acts, and executive orders chipped away at Ojibwe reservations from the outside, the policy of allotment effectively broke up tribal control of land inside those reservations. Under the guise of granting individual Indians the rights and opportunities of private land ownership, the U.S. government enacted the allotment policy to break up the tribal control of land within reservation borders and give chunks of land within reservations to individual tribal members. Left-over "surplus" land was opened to white settlement under homestead laws. The Dawes Act (1887) enabled allotment of tribal lands nationwide; the Nelson Act (1889) brought this policy to bear in Minnesota. Allotment placed control of the land with individuals and families rather than with the tribe. In spite of a twenty-five-year trust period in which allotments were not to be sold, speculators bought most of the allotments within a few years. Lands held by Ojibwe were illegally taxed and then lost in tax forfeitures. Store clerks and traders claimed

Dawes & Nelson Acts

Allotments

Henry Rice negotiated Red Lake land cessions and allotment for all other Ojibwe tribes on behalf of the U.S. government in the late nineteenth century. He was one of Minnesota's most beloved politicians but one of the most despised in Ojibwe country.

Red Lake chiefs,
1889

allotments in lieu of payment from Ojibwe customers for
trumped-up merchandise charges.[27]

The policy of allotment drastically changed land ownership among the Ojibwe in Minnesota. Leech Lake Indians
owned less than 4 percent of their own reservation when
the allotment policy ended in 1934. Mille Lacs Indians
owned less than 7 percent of theirs. White Earth Indians
owned less than 10 percent of their reservation.

Legal claims followed over the years—some resolved,
many not. The White Earth Land Settlement Act of 1986
was a major legislative attempt to clear titles and compen-
sate the Ojibwe, but it was fraught with controversy. Much
of the land at White Earth and Leech Lake still has clouded
title or so many people claiming title that it cannot be legally sold, transferred, or developed.[28]

At Mille Lacs, tribal members were under constant pressure to relocate to the White Earth Reservation. Under government policy, they could claim allotments only at White

Ojibwe receiving allotments, White Earth Indian Agency, 1890

Earth until 1926. The local sheriff even burned down a hundred Indian homes at Mille Lacs in 1901, telling the residents to move to White Earth. By the time the government allowed the Mille Lacs Ojibwe to take allotments at Mille Lacs in 1926, the plots were reduced to five-acre homesteads and more than two-thirds of the population had relocated.

The Red Lake Reservation was a special case in Minnesota. Because it was the most remote tribe in the state (being farthest north and west), Red Lake retained a huge 3 million-acre land parcel when the government stopped making treaties in 1871. The U.S. government used the Nelson Act to try to gain land cessions from Red Lake and simultaneously implement allotment throughout Minnesota. Red Lake chiefs agreed to a land cession but not to allotment. Even today, individual Indians do not own land at Red Lake. The tribe holds all land collectively, and parcels are designated as homesteads with no rights of ownership. All the other tribes in Minnesota endured allotment and the land loss that accompanied the policy.

The treaty period and the formation of reservations in Minnesota was unbearably hard for the Ojibwe. The Anishinaabe descended into abject poverty, lost most of their

The Battle of Sugar Point, 1898

For the most part, Ojibwe resistance to government policies was peaceful. But there was one significant exception. On September 15, 1898, U.S. Deputy Marshal Robert Morrison and U.S. Indian Agent Arthur M. Tinker took Leech Lake elder Hole in the Day (Bagone-giizhig) into custody in a bootlegging case. Hole in the Day was a staunch diplomatic opponent of many government policies, and many Ojibwe feared that his arrest was politically motivated, especially when they learned that he would be transported to Duluth rather than brought to the Indian agency at Walker. Several Ojibwe from Sugar Point and Bear Island on the Leech Lake Reservation attacked Morrison and Tinker and helped Hole in the Day escape.[v]

Hole in the Day (Bagone-giizhig) of Leech Lake, 1899. His necklace is made from carbine casings collected from the site of the Battle of Sugar Point.

Major Melville C. Wilkinson, General John M. Bacon, and a detachment of around a hundred soldiers from the 3rd Infantry Regiment boarded steamers and came to Bear Island on Leech Lake on October 5 with the intent of re-arresting Hole in the Day. On disembarking, one of the soldiers accidentally discharged his rifle, and a large group of Ojibwe hiding nearby thought they were being attacked and fired back. Six soldiers, including Major Wilkinson, were killed. Ten more were wounded. One Indian police officer was also killed. None of the Leech Lake Ojibwe died.

The entire event was resolved through diplomatic channels. In one of the most astounding comments on the matter, Secretary of the Interior Cornelius Newton Bliss wrote, "The Indians were prompted to their outbreak by the wrongs committed against them and chafed under unfair treatment. They now will go back to their homes and live peaceably if the whites will treat them fairly, which is very likely, as the whites were thoroughly impressed with the stand taken by the Indians. In this respect the outbreak has taught them a lesson."

The Battle of Sugar Point was the last military conflict between a tribe and the U.S. government. Revered Leech Lake elder Emma Bear, the last known survivor of the battle, passed away in 2001 at the age of 103.

U.S. Army troops from the Battle of Sugar Point, 1898

Ojibwe family at Grand Marais, 1900

land, and watched the dismantling of their long-standing warrior and political culture. At the same time, the U.S. government, religious missionaries, and educators sought to assimilate native peoples, attacking the very fabric of Ojibwe society, language, and culture. Change eventually came to the Ojibwe in the 1930s, as part of the Indian New Deal.

The Indian New Deal

When John Collier assumed control of the Bureau of Indian Affairs during the Great Depression, he engineered the most substantial change in U.S. Indian policy to date. The BIA went from being the supervisory agency that oversaw all Indian matters in the country to being an advisory agency that empowered and assisted tribes in their dealings with the U.S. government. It was a profound change.

The biggest part of Collier's policy shift came in 1934

John Collier

with passage of the Indian Reorganization Act, also known as the Wheeler-Howard Bill. It was part of a series of reforms sometimes called the Indian New Deal. The Indian Reorganization Act (IRA) ended the policy of allotment and enabled tribes to establish modern tribal governments with their own representatives. The courts of Indian offenses, Indian police, and Indian agents were no longer needed. Indians would manage their own internal affairs, governing themselves and managing their own land. All of the Ojibwe tribes in Minnesota voted to accept reorganization under the act and created modern constitution-based democratic tribal governments, much as they remain today.[29]

One entity formed under the IRA in 1934 was the Minnesota Chippewa Tribe (MCT), which represented all of the Ojibwe reservations in Minnesota except Red Lake. The driving concept behind the MCT was that each member reservation had the same language and culture and that a combined tribal government operation would reduce waste and bureaucratic duplications. The result was almost the opposite, however: all of the member tribes had their own reservation business committees to manage local affairs, but those local reservation governments needed approval from

Indian police force, White Earth Reservation, 1908

the MCT and the BIA for all major actions, from funding initiatives to tribal enrollment. Hampered by the bureaucracy at the MCT, some tribes have sought to disband the organization or withdraw from it. But without approval from the BIA and all member tribes in the MCT, constitutional reform and withdrawal have been stopped every time.[30]

Cons of IRA

While the Indian Reorganization Act was largely positive, it created some new tensions in Minnesota's Ojibwe communities. In 1934, the Mille Lacs Ojibwe were recognized and organized as a sovereign native nation in the eyes of the federal government, along with the other Ojibwe reservations in Minnesota. However, the separate and autonomous Ojibwe communities at Sandy Lake, East Lake, Lake Lena, and Isle were not recognized as independent under the act. They were simply lumped together with Mille Lacs as communities within the same reservation. Sandy Lake, which had always been a sovereign group with its own leadership tradition and reservation, now found itself a smaller and less integral part of a larger Indian political structure. Its traditional leaders no longer made primary decisions about their community. Within the Mille Lacs government, Sandy Lake had a district representative but not autonomous control. The IRA thus created intratribal tensions at the same time that it reaffirmed the land tenure and sovereignty of Mille Lacs and the surrounding Ojibwe communities. The issue of independence for various Indian communities in the Mille Lacs Reservation is still unresolved for many Indians enrolled there, although changes in the current political configuration of the reservation now seem unlikely.

The work of crafting native governments under the Indian Reorganization Act is ongoing. In Minnesota, Ojibwe tribal governments remain modeled on the American corporate governance system. Generally, they do not contain attributes of traditional Ojibwe leadership structure and procedure. However, there are some notable exceptions.

The Red Lake Reservation brought all of its hereditary tribal chiefs into the government as advisers, and to this day they sit at all council meetings to advise the council and participate in all proceedings. In 2009, White Earth adopted major constitutional reforms that try to incorporate older ideals and values as part of its government structure, although these reforms have not been approved by the MCT or the BIA.[31]

Ojibwe boys at Mille Lacs, 1930

adaptations

The IRA was a positive development for Indian self-rule and far less obtrusive than the direct management of the Bureau of Indian Affairs, but it also established quasi-democratic institutions that undermined older Indian ideas of leadership, representation, culture, and justice. Post-IRA tribal governments were an improvement over BIA control but were riddled with major structural problems. These problems include no proper voting and recall procedures and a judicial branch appointed by and serving at the pleasure of the tribal council. There was no balance of power or accountability woven into the new constitutional frameworks. The substantive change introduced with the Indian Reorganization Act was that Indians had the power to represent Indian interests and manage affairs within reservation boundaries. The Ojibwe did not regain their traditional leadership structure in 1934, but tribal sovereignty was on the rise.

What Sovereignty Means

The underpinnings of tribal sovereignty, treaty rights, and modern casino development are all deeply embedded in American law, which makes them paradoxically very well documented but poorly understood by most

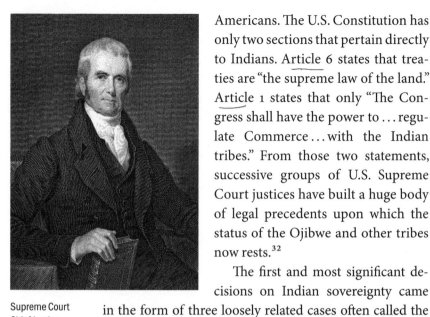

Supreme Court
Chief Justice
John Marshall

U.S. Congress + courts

tricky

Americans. The U.S. Constitution has only two sections that pertain directly to Indians. Article 6 states that treaties are "the supreme law of the land." Article 1 states that only "The Congress shall have the power to . . . regulate Commerce . . . with the Indian tribes." From those two statements, successive groups of U.S. Supreme Court justices have built a huge body of legal precedents upon which the status of the Ojibwe and other tribes now rests.[32]

The first and most significant decisions on Indian sovereignty came in the form of three loosely related cases often called the Marshall Trilogy. They get their name from John Marshall, chief justice of the Supreme Court in the 1830s. The three cases (*Cherokee Nation v. Georgia, Worcester v. Georgia*, and *State v. George Tassels*) used the scanty language in the U.S. Constitution to create the concept of *domestic dependent nations*. The legal ruling was that tribes were in fact nations, putting their laws and actions above those of individuals, states, or county governments. In *Cherokee*, for example, the court ruled that the State of Georgia had no authority to relocate the Cherokee Indians because the tribe was a *nation* that had existed before the United States. At the same time, the rulings also contained very paternalistic language about tribal nations, calling them *dependent* on the United States.

The court's rulings appeared to be in the favor of the Indians. The Cherokee could not be forced from their lands by a state government, for example. But the long-term effects served to undermine tribal sovereignty. Using the words "little red children" and "great white father," the court made it clear that the U.S. government maintained significant power over Indians. Tribal sovereignty existed, but at the pleasure of the federal government.

Over the next one hundred years, the courts and Congress further defined and limited the nature of tribal sovereignty but never eliminated it. In *Ex Parte Crow Dog* (1883), the court reinforced the legal precedent in the Marshall Trilogy that state (or, in this case, territorial) government had no jurisdiction over Indians. A Lakota Indian named Crow Dog had killed another Indian and was punished in a traditional tribal council. The council's decision was to banish Crow Dog and his family for four generations and to mandate that Crow Dog care for the widow of the man he had killed. Dakota Territory officials felt Crow Dog was getting away with murder in spite of his punishment by tribal custom, so they tried and convicted him of murder in territorial court. The U.S. Supreme Court overturned his conviction because the territory had no jurisdiction over tribes, just as a state or territory had no jurisdiction over other nations.

White outrage continued after the ruling in *Crow Dog*, however, and Congress did exercise its "plenary authority" over tribes, passing a critical piece of legislation called the Major Crimes Act in 1885. For non-Indians, most major crimes were (and still are) exclusively a matter of state jurisdiction. Each state outlawed murder, for example, but had different criminal codes, which is why even today some states have a death penalty and others do not. Murder was never a federal offense. For Indians, the Major Crimes Act changed that, making federal crimes of murder, rape, arson, and other major offences between Indians on Indian land. The act was amended many times but still remains the basis for criminal law on Indian reservations today. Subsequent rulings in *U.S. v. Kagama, Lone Wolf v. Hitchcock, U.S. v. Celestine,* and other cases affirmed the basic concept that the U.S. government could do what it wanted to tribal sovereignty but that state governments could not.

These are the essential concepts in the law that inform and affirm the unique sovereign status of tribes in the United States, including the Ojibwe.

Public Law 280

Tribes had authority over their own reservations, free from all but federal interference, until passage of Public Law 280 in 1953. This was a federal congressional act, but it only applied to tribes in five states—Oregon, Nebraska, California, Wisconsin, and Minnesota. Eleven other states were later added to the list. In spite of its seemingly small scope, Public Law 280 had a substantial and long-lasting impact on the Ojibwe in Minnesota.[33]

After passage of Public Law 280, Minnesota and other states covered by the act would assume all criminal and limited civil jurisdiction over Indians. Minnesota's complex web of criminal law now formally applied to Indians for the first time in history. In the 1950s, tribal governments were new, weak, and unaware of Public Law 280's implications. The law passed without the consent of Minnesota tribal leaders, with one very notable exception.

Red Lake Tribal Chairman Roger Jourdain was an especially shrewd and savvy leader. He constantly scrutinized every legislative agenda and U.S. government action. Jourdain immediately recognized Public Law 280 as an intrusion into Red Lake's sovereignty, intervened before the bill was introduced to Congress, and successfully fought to have Red Lake exempted from the law.

Red Lake developed and maintained its own criminal code, court system, and police force through auspices of the Bureau of Indian Affairs. Today the federal government intervenes and assumes jurisdiction there over major crimes, but the State of Minnesota has no authority at Red Lake. That is why, for example, when a school shooting at Red Lake occurred in 2005, federal law enforcement agencies investigated and state agencies had no jurisdiction. The Bois Forte Reservation was initially subject to Public Law 280 but succeeded in getting an exemption in 1975. It also maintains its own courts, police, and legal code.

Bois Forte and Red Lake are now exploring ways to use their courts to exert jurisdiction over major crimes as well. In 2009, for example, a Bois Forte tribal member burned down the tribal headquarters and was charged with arson under the Major Crimes Act. Bois Forte also charged him with arson in tribal court. The dual charge was not double jeopardy because the United States and Bois Forte are separate sovereigns under the law. This tactic has the potential to expand tribal jurisdiction and weaken the Major Crimes Act.

At the same time, pressure is mounting for a repeal of Public Law 280 or a case-by-case exemption for the rest of Minnesota's Ojibwe reservations. As tribes have become better educated about sovereignty and the law and better funded, most have begun to develop their own court systems and police forces. As of 2009, Fond du Lac was the only tribe in Minnesota that did not have its own court. A few have negotiated memoranda of agreement with state, county, and municipal law enforcement agencies. Minnesota tribes have also had success in legal challenges to the civil authority of states over Indians in Public Law 280, as demonstrated by *Bryan v. Itasca County* and other cases.[34]

Termination

While the Ojibwe of Minnesota were deeply affected by Public Law 280, they narrowly escaped the effects of legislation intended to terminate tribal sovereignty altogether. The policy of termination formally began in 1954, although it had been debated and experimented with previously. Every tribe in the United States was to be systematically terminated one by one—tribal governments, land, and members would be completely absorbed into mainstream America. The policy was a disaster wherever it was implemented.[35]

When the Menominee of Wisconsin were terminated, their self-sufficient logging businesses were closed. Tribal land became taxable and much of it was sold to pay those taxes. Termination opponent and Menominee tribal member Ada Deer said, "It was like burning your house down to stay warm in winter." The people became far more impoverished than they were prior to the policy. It cost the government more money in welfare payments after termination than it had cost the BIA in tribal support funding prior to termination. The Menominee were eventually reinstated.

While the policy itself ended before any Minnesota Ojibwe were affected, results of the policy were disastrous for terminated tribes such as the Klamath, Catawba, and Coquille. The policy further deepened Indian feelings of distrust of and betrayal by the U.S. government, adding to the fervor of Indian activism in the 1960s and 1970s and further isolating tribes from American political life.

Spearing fish,
1925

Supporters of Ojibwe treaty rights in Wisconsin, ca. 1990. The dispute started in Wisconsin although the treaty area covered parts of Minnesota, too.

Treaty Rights

Since the 1970s, tribes have become proactive in testing the limits of their sovereignty. In 1974, an Ojibwe named Fred Tribble violated Wisconsin state game laws by spearing fish on lands that his tribe had ceded to the U.S. government. Tribble claimed that a land cession treaty signed by the Ojibwe contained terms that allowed him to do so. After the nine-year appeal of his case (*Lac Courte Oreilles v. Wisconsin*), the federal circuit court of appeals upheld his claim. Treaties were the supreme law of the land. Only Congress can interfere with treaty rights, and Congress had not done so in that case.[36]

Tribal fisherman Vincent Wolfe at North Twin Lake, 1990, waiting by the barricade erected by police to protect Ojibwe tribal members exercising treaty rights

With the Tribble case, Ojibwe people throughout Wisconsin and Minnesota looked back at the treaties their ancestors had negotiated in the 1800s. Most contained specific agreements about the harvest of natural resources on all ancestral lands—both reservation lands and lands ceded to

White Earth elder George "Joe Bush" Fairbanks, offering tobacco and prayers as tribal and state conservation programs stock sturgeon in area waters. All Minnesota Ojibwe reservations actively stock fish and manage their natural resources for sustainable harvest.

the U.S. government. In Wisconsin and Minnesota, when Ojibwe sought to exercise treaty rights by harvesting fish, ugly protests sprang up. Anti–fish harvesting protesters in Wisconsin marketed "treaty beer" to fund their campaigns against treaty rights. Many carried signs saying, "Timber Niggers Go Home," "Save a Walleye, Spear an Indian," and "Save Two Walleye, Spear a Pregnant Squaw." Pipe bombs were found at boat landings, and hundreds of protesters were arrested as they charged tribal fishermen over police barricades.

On the Mille Lacs Ojibwe reservation in central Minnesota, tensions rose when state and municipal governments attempted to enforce state fishing regulations on tribal members. These efforts only strengthened tribal solidarity and the search to affirm treaty rights. The contest over access to and use of Mille Lacs Lake went all the way to the U.S. Supreme Court in 1999. In *Minnesota v. Mille Lacs Band of Chippewa Indians*, the court again ruled that treaty rights and tribal sovereignty were unaffected by state laws and regulations.

Indian Child Welfare Act

Although the U.S. government's relationship with tribes has often been oppositional, or at least strained, the pendulum has swung in the other direction at times, especially after the period of heightened American Indian activism in the 1970s. Tribes have been very appreciative of two federal acts: the Indian Child Welfare Act and the Native American Graves Protection and Repatriation Act.

The Indian Child Welfare Act (ICWA) of 1978 sought to address problems in adoption and foster care of Anishinaabe children. Expert testimony presented at the legislative hearings for the act included surveys conducted by the Association on American Indian Affairs and other organizations. These surveys indicated that as many as 35 percent of Anishinaabe children were separated from their homes by adoption or foster care. In Minnesota, up to 25 percent of the infant Indian population was being adopted. Minnesota's out-of-home placement rate for Indians was five times the rate for nonnative children. More than 90 percent of adoption and foster placements in Minnesota were with non-Indians. The trend was undercutting parents' authority in raising their own children and disconnecting Anishinaabe youth from their families, reservations, and culture. Social service agencies were plagued with oversight and procedural problems. Most of the native kids removed from their homes never had a social worker visit those homes. Racial bias was prevalent. Many tribal members were terrified of losing their children, not because they were bad parents but because they were Indian.[37]

The Indian Child Welfare Act was the first serious legislative attempt to alleviate the problem. It mandated that state courts and county social service case agencies follow ranked priorities in placing children removed from their homes. Children were to be placed (1) following the preference of the child and parent, (2) with extended family, (3) with other tribal members, and (4) with other Indians. The ICWA also required that agencies notify tribes of cases affecting their tribal members. It further granted tribal courts and agencies the right to intervene in their children's welfare.

ICWA was a big step in the right direction, but there were many problems with the law. First, it provided no teeth. There were no fines, sanctions, or punishments for individuals or agencies that did not comply. It was also difficult for caseworkers to know if a child was Indian, to determine what tribe the child was enrolled in (or even if the child was enrolled), and to find qualified native homes for placement of children. Canadian Indians living in the United States and Indians with no known tribal affiliation were not covered by the act as they were not "federally recognized."

The act also provided no means or guidance for education or training of social service workers about Anishinaabe culture, history, language, or even the act itself. Often tribes received no notice, or a late notice, of a child needing placement. By the time they tried to intervene and advocate, the affected children had already been removed from their homes. Years after the act, trends were barely affected: whereas 74 percent of foster care placements in Minnesota involved a house visit by a social worker, only 29 percent of the Indian foster care removals had a social service worker visit the home.

Today, communication between tribal and county agencies has greatly improved. The State of Minnesota and tribal governments also signed a memorandum of agreement that obligates the state to pay for foster care placements ordered by tribal courts. The effects of the ICWA have been welcome but modest, and much more needs to be done to ensure tribal involvement in the process, racial sensitivity training and cultural education for county social service workers, reduction in unnecessary removals of Indian children, and connection of removed children to their communities and culture.

NAGPRA

In 1990, Congress passed major legislation to protect and repatriate Indian funerary and cultural artifacts. Protest was growing in native communities and the general population about the robbing of native graves. Tribes were being denied access to sacred items critical to the survival of certain ceremonies. In addition, many Indian skeletons were being kept by government agencies for "scientific" purposes. The Smithsonian Institution alone held more than two hundred thousand Indian skeletons. The Native American Graves Protection and Repatriation Act (NAGPRA) was designed to stop looting and give tribes the power to claim their own funerary and sacred items.[38]

As a result of NAGPRA, the White Earth Reservation in northwestern Minnesota received two repatriated ceremonial drums—one held by a church and one held by a university museum. The repatriated items were essential to revitalizing traditional drum culture at White Earth, which had been silent for decades before the act was passed. The Bois Forte Reservation has also received high-profile repatriations. Funerary items and skeletons have been returned to Minnesota Ojibwe tribes.

The main problem with NAGPRA is that it does not go far enough. It applies only to federal agencies and agencies receiving federal funds. It does not affect private collectors and institutions.

Issues such as the repatriation of Indian remains and artifacts and the exercise of treaty rights challenge the Minnesota Ojibwe and the rest of the country to gain a deeper understanding of the legal status of tribes and their sovereignty. Tribal self-rule is not a new gift to Indians based on political correctness or affirmative action ideals. Tribal sovereignty is inherent and preexists the creation of the United States—a basic concept that is deeply embedded and affirmed in the U.S. Constitution and every major Indian court case. For tribes, that sovereignty is the cornerstone of their survival as unique political, economic, and cultural entities. For everyone else, tribal sovereignty is a litmus test for the integrity of American democracy. Renowned tribal law expert Felix S. Cohen provided an apt analogy: "Like the

Relocation

While the Ojibwe struggled to establish sovereignty and treaty rights on reservations in the twentieth century, they also faced pressure to leave their homes. Relocation was a policy designed to get Indians off reservations and permanently moved to urban areas. The idea was that native people could then enjoy economic opportunity and better assimilate into American society.[vi]

A piecemeal experiment began in 1948. Then, from 1953 to 1960, the commissioner of Indian Affairs issued a mandate, supported by congressional funding in 1956. Relocation provided one-way transportation for Indian families to urban areas and rental assistance for the first month of relocation. The policy had dramatic effects on the Ojibwe in Minnesota. Under the program, thousands of Ojibwe relocated to Minneapolis, St. Paul, and Duluth. Even today, 35 percent of Minnesota's total native population is located in those three cities as a direct result of this policy.[vii]

Relocation succeeded in moving Indians, but it failed to provide jobs, housing, and other economic opportunities. Indian unemployment rates in urban areas during relocation were as high as 50 percent. Relocation was abandoned in 1960 for being too expensive, but the damage had been done. As of the year 2000, unemployment had declined to 22 percent for the urban Indian population, but that was still higher than the unemployment rates for Indians on reservations and much higher than the overall state unemployment rate of 4 percent. During the Great Depression the unemployment rate rose more than 15 percent, but for the Ojibwe people in Minnesota it has never been below 20 percent since the creation of the first reservation in the state. For the Minnesota Ojibwe, a great depression began with the first reservation. It has never ended.[viii]

It is important to note that for urban Ojibwe connection to their home communities is vitally important. Almost all urban Ojibwe travel back and forth frequently, vote in tribal elections, and have their funerals on their home reservations. Most of the tribes have established urban tribal offices for outreach to those constituents.

miner's canary, the Indian marks the shifts from fresh air to poison gas in our political atmosphere; and our treatment of Indians, even more than our treatment of other minorities, reflects the rise and fall in our democratic faith." The Constitution says that treaties are "the supreme law of the land." It is high time all Americans honor Supreme Court Justice Hugo Black's statement on tribal sovereignty: "Great nations like great men, must keep their word."[39]

Indian Gaming

In addition to treaty rights, tribes have discovered and tested other critical areas of the law to their benefit. In *Bryan v.*

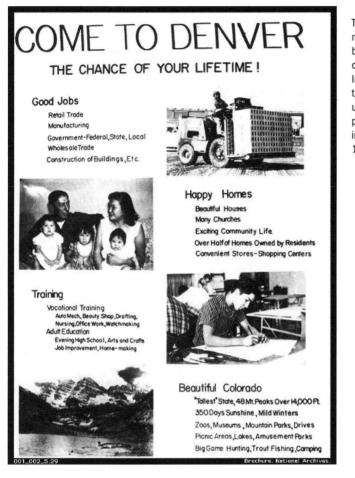

COME TO DENVER

THE CHANCE OF YOUR LIFETIME !

Good Jobs
Retail Trade
Manufacturing
Government-Federal,State, Local
WholesaleTrade
Construction of Buildings,Etc.

Happy Homes
Beautiful Houses
Many Churches
Exciting Community Life
Over Half of Homes Owned by Residents
Convenient Stores-Shopping Centers

Training
Vocational Training
Auto Mech, Beauty Shop,Drafting,
Nursing,Office Work,Watchmaking
Adult Education
Evening High School, Arts and Crafts
Job Improvement, Home- making

Beautiful Colorado
"Tallest" State, 48 Mt. Peaks Over 14,000 Ft.
350 Days Sunshine, Mild Winters
Zoos, Museums, Mountain Parks, Drives
Picnic Areas,Lakes, Amusement Parks
Big Game Hunting,Trout Fishing ,Camping

001_002_5.29   Brochure. National Archives.

The U.S. government circulated brochures like this one to Minnesota Indians to entice them to move to urban areas as part of relocation initiatives in the 1950s.

Itasca County (1976), Ojibwe Indians Helen and Russell Bryan successfully proved that they should not be subject to state or county tax on their mobile home. The mobile home was on land held in federal trust for the Leech Lake Reservation, and the Bryans were enrolled members of the Minnesota Chippewa Tribe. This was a critical case because it solidified earlier court decisions limiting state regulation of reservation affairs, even in the face of federal legislation that granted greater authority to states on tribal land.[40]

Shorty after and in part because of *Bryan,* the Florida Seminole Indians began developing tribal gaming and gambling enterprises. Gaming and gambling are not governed by federal laws. Some states, like Nevada and South Dakota, have legalized many forms of gambling, while others, like Minnesota, have not. The Seminole Indians of Florida simply paid no attention to the state's gaming laws, which allowed church bingo but nothing more. They developed a high-stakes bingo operation on tribal land. The local sheriff tried to shut it down, but the tribe filed for an injunction, which was appealed all the way to the Fifth Circuit Court of Appeals.

Casinos

The 1981 decision in *Seminole Tribe of Florida v. Robert Butterworth* upheld the right of the Seminole to develop gaming operations without regard to state laws. It was another sovereignty victory for tribal governments and a huge eye-opener for tribes in states that had not legalized casino gambling. Legal challenges to tribal gaming continued after *Seminole v. Butterworth*. However, in 1987 the U.S. Supreme Court ruled in *California v. Cabazon Band of Mission Indians* that California could not regulate gaming on Indian land when it allowed gaming elsewhere in the state. After *Cabazon*, tribal gaming proliferated. Within two years, every Ojibwe reservation in Minnesota developed some type of high-stakes bingo or casino-style gaming operation.[41]

The U.S. government, under the Indian Gaming Regulatory Act, did require states and tribes to negotiate compacts, or agreements, governing the type and nature of their gaming enterprises. The law also clarified that the ruling in *Cabazon* would apply to tribes in all states, regardless of other federal statutes like Public Law 280. In spite of the required compacts, the rapid growth of tribal gaming continued. Minnesota signed twenty-two tribal gaming compacts in 1989. Legally, states cannot refuse to sign compacts. Nor can states insist that tribes share gaming revenue with them.

The Impact of Casinos

Tribal gaming operations in Minnesota have had a profound effect on the Ojibwe. Unemployment rates dropped from 50 percent in many communities to 20 percent in just a few years. Tribes reinvested proceeds in business development, education, and social service programs for tribal members.[42]

The impact of gaming on tribal members varied depending on location. White Earth had more than twenty thousand tribal members and one casino, so, aside from job creation, the impact of gaming on the daily lives of tribal members was not pronounced. Mille Lacs had only three thousand tribal members and two much larger casinos. That, together with a sound business plan, allowed Mille Lacs to develop a retirement plan and health insurance for all members, four new schools, a hospital, new dance halls for all the band's ceremonial drums, and aggressive reinvestment in housing, tribal infrastructure, and social services. Most tribal members are supportive of the new revenue stream and resurgent tribal economic and political power. Nevertheless, rising tides have not lifted

Fortune Bay Casino Resort, operated by the Bois Forte Band of Ojibwe (Nett Lake)

all boats. As of 2000, Ojibwe people in Minnesota were still disproportionately poor. Thirty percent of Minnesota Indians from all tribes were below the poverty line, compared to 5 percent of the overall state population. Unemployment also remained high, with 20 percent of Indians being unemployed versus 4 percent of the overall state population.[43]

Many Ojibwe worry about negative impacts of gaming, since tribal members patronize the casinos in large numbers. Increased rates of gambling addiction, exposure to secondhand cigarette smoke, and what many view as an unhealthy and untraditional environment in the casinos are among the greatest worries. There is also a common misconception among non-Indians that "all Indians are rich from casinos." This perception has led many granting agencies and regular citizens to believe that tribes do not need outside help in fighting poverty or in developing programs. The influx of money to tribes through gaming has created its own problems, causing tension between tribal members and leading to accusations of mismanagement and embezzlement. Some of those accusations are well founded; others are not.

Another highly contested issue surrounding casino development is per capita payments. Under per capita payments, a percentage of casino profits or a fixed amount of money is distributed to every member of a tribe. Tribes such as White Earth will probably never be able to offer payments, since they have so many tribal members relative to their gaming income. However, Ojibwe communities with small populations and large casino operations, such as Mille Lacs, Grand Portage, and Fond du Lac, pay a portion of their casino proceeds directly to tribal members. The payments are relatively small, numbering in the hundreds of dollars every month, but they create huge dilemmas for tribal governments and members. Members want

per capita payments

the payments and pressure or elect leaders who promise to increase them. These demands often put undue stress on the bottom line for tribes, stretching margins to make per capita payments and diverting revenue from deserving programs, including health, education, and housing. Tribal officials are caught in the middle. They find it politically impossible to reduce per capita payments but difficult to expand other businesses and programs when significant funds are diverted to paying tribal members.

where does the money go?

Some people feel that per capita payments do more harm than good. For example, tribes often put aside per capita payments for minors and give them large lump-sum payments at age eighteen. This sudden influx of spending power can accelerate negative behavior for some youth, who want to party with the largest check they have ever received, and it often provides a disincentive for further education or career development. In addition, tribal members who used to augment their income and feed their families by harvesting wild rice, berries, fish, and gardening now receive per capita payments and are far less likely to participate in those traditional lifeways, taking another step away from healthy living and further eroding traditional Ojibwe culture. Moreover, Ojibwe tribes that can't really afford to make per capita payments have actually been exploring ways to cut spending on social services and education in response to member demands for casino income.

more harm than good

The development and growth of tribal gaming operations for the Minnesota Ojibwe have generated economic and political power for tribes like nothing else since the Indian Reorganization Act of 1934. Yet that power brings a price, creating both internal and external strife. The real test will come over the following decades as the discussion shifts from whether or not tribes should have casinos to determining the most sensible and effective ways to manage gaming revenue for the best benefit to the people.

strife

Legislation and Events

Indian Citizenship Act	1924
Homestead Allotments allowed in Mille Lacs	1926
Chippewa National Forest created	1928
Indian Reorganization Act	1934
Public Law 280	1953
Relocation	1953–60
Termination	1953–64
Indian Child Welfare Act	1978
American Indian Religious Freedom Act	1978
Indian Gaming Regulatory Act	1988
Native American Graves Protection and Repatriation Act	1990

Community, Activism, and the Ojibwe in Minnesota

The Ojibwe became U.S. citizens in 1924 with passage of the Indian Citizenship Act. In Minnesota, the Anishinaabe gained the right to vote shortly thereafter, within the living memory of many Ojibwe people today. In spite of that notable development, most Ojibwe saw themselves as tribal citizens first and foremost. Even today, many Ojibwe people actively participate in tribal elections but abstain from voting in municipal, state, and federal elections. They see themselves as dual citizens, but their interest and trust leans mostly toward their own tribal governments.[44]

Within reservations, Ojibwe tribal members identify with specific communities even more than they do with the reservation to which they belong. At Red Lake, for example, it makes all the difference in the world if someone is from Ponemah or Red Lake village. Each place has its own cluster of families, traditional chiefs, history, and cultural practice. For instance, a person from Ponemah would certainly have a traditional Ojibwe funeral, while a person from Red Lake village almost equally certainly would have a Catholic funeral. No matter where a person lived or worked, his or her funeral would almost invariably take place on the home reservation in the home community. When there is a funeral at Ponemah, most families help cook and bring food to the service, not just because they often knew the deceased but because they are all part of the same community. Connection to place is a critical surviving attribute of Ojibwe culture.

This strong connection to place is only now starting to change—and only in some places. Residents of Bena on the

Leech Lake Reservation complain that the tribe itself is orchestrating that change. For generations, each village was home only to certain families. But the tribe is now building houses for members anywhere on the reservation, without regard for community customs and structure. There are now families from Sugar Point, Onigum, Federal Dam, and Inger living in Bena. The composition of the community is changing, along with its sense of solidarity, largely because of the tribal housing program. Other reservations have more carefully reinforced community cohesion. At Red Lake, that sense is strongest. No one at Red Lake owns land, but families can inherit occupation rights to plots.

Sense of community shows itself in many ways among the Ojibwe in Minnesota. Almost every community on every reservation sponsors a powwow, which is proudly attended by most of the families from that community and many visitors. Community care and pride are powerful and evident at powwows and elsewhere. One of the road signs on the way to Ponemah, for example, reads "Home of the Ojibway Language." Ponemah's status as the place with the highest Ojibwe fluency rate in the United States is a source of community-wide pride, even for nonspeakers.

Billboard on the road to Ponemah (Red Lake Nation)

Ojibwe identification with reservation and community is beautiful and powerful. However, it has a nasty side too in the bitterly contentious world of tribal politics. Political conflicts predate reservations but strengthened after formation of tribal governments during the Indian New Deal. The draft constitutions handed to Minnesota's Ojibwe tribes as part of the Indian Reorganization Act in 1934 contained no clear separation of powers. Tribal governments tended to be based more on strong people than strong institutions. Judges were appointed at the pleasure of the tribal council or the tribal chair—even the judges who oversaw election disputes and grievances against the tribal chair. There were no clear voting and recall procedures.

As long as tribal leaders had impeccable integrity and transparent financial operations, all was well. But when members questioned leadership integrity or discovered complicated finances, accusations flew and people fought. Some tribal administrations have seethed with infighting and anger. Recent efforts at meaningful constitutional reform show promise, but much work remains to be done in modifying and strengthening tribal institutions. That work is hampered by a general tribal distrust of any strong institution, a lack of vision on the part of some tribal leaders in developing policies and programs, and an extraordinarily cumbersome process for reform, especially within the Minnesota Chippewa Tribe. The MCT has to approve any such changes for all of Minnesota's reservations except Red Lake.[45]

Frequently tribal members are so focused on community and tribal politics that Ojibwe voices are rarely heard in county, state, or federal political theaters. There have been some notable exceptions. Leech Lake member Elaine Fleming became the first Ojibwe mayor in the state when she was elected by the citizens of Cass Lake. Leech Lake member Skip Finn was elected to the Minnesota state senate. Leech Lake members Joseph Day, Jennifer Wind-

Reyes, and others have served on school boards. Still, for the most part, Ojibwe people have been uninterested in participating in or representing their people in government outside their reservations. A sometimes charged racial climate makes it hard for many native people to gain political traction with whites. In addition, Ojibwe people rarely hold the kinds of jobs, as lawyers, bankers, and so on, that often lead to political office. Yet the need and potential for Ojibwe participation in county, state, and federal politics is undeniable.

AIM

Minnesota Ojibwe people have made their voices heard on the national stage, but usually in opposition to the American political process rather than as a part of that process. The clearest example of this is the American Indian Movement (AIM), founded by Ojibwe and other Indians in Minneapolis in 1968. AIM was catapulted to national fame for its poignant protests of federal Indian policy and its marches

Leech Lake Ojibwe member Dennis Banks, cofounder of the American Indian Movement

White Earth Ojibwe member Clyde Bellecourt, cofounder of the American Indian Movement

and takeovers, including takeover of the federal prison at Alcatraz Island near San Francisco, California, in 1969 (which AIM members participated in but did not originally organize), the Trail of Broken Treaties march from California to Washington, DC in 1972, takeover of the Bureau of Indian Affairs in Washington, DC in 1972, burning of the courthouse in Custer, South Dakota, in 1973, and takeover of the Wounded Knee Trading Post on the Pine Ridge Reservation in South Dakota in 1973. As a result of those protests, many Americans heard, felt, and understood Indian discontent with government policies for the first time, even though the civil disobedience did little to change policy.[46]

AIM's greatest achievements are the ones for which the

Trail of Broken Treaties (handwritten margin note)

American Indian Movement march to commemorate five hundred years of resistance, 1992

organization is less well known but which began in Minnesota. AIM was initially created to deal with Indian urbanization and poverty in Minneapolis. It started the AIM Legal Rights Center in 1968, which provided free legal counsel, advice, and representation to Indians in Minnesota. More than thirty thousand people have been served by the legal center to date. AIM also founded the AIM Patrol in 1968, which initially sought to police the police, document cases of police brutality and racial profiling, assist Indians with legal grievances, and advocate for victims of crimes. The AIM Patrol evolved over time. In 1986, a serial killer was targeting Indian women in Minneapolis, and the AIM Patrol provided free protective escorts for native women who needed to walk or ride to work, school, and shopping centers. AIM also developed the American Indian Opportunities Industrialization Center in 1979, which has successfully offered job training and placement for urban and reservation Anishinaabe.[47]

The American Indian Movement also provided innovative leadership in education by pioneering the first Indian culture–based K-12 school in Minnesota. The Heart of the Earth Survival School was created in 1971, and to date it has graduated more Indians than all of the other Minneapolis-area schools combined. Heart of the Earth has undergone some serious struggles, but its achievements in serving urban Indian youth and inspiring other tribal school initiatives are remarkable.

In recent years, AIM has been protesting the use of Indian names and icons as sports mascots and joined with other organizations in creating the National Coalition on Racism in Sports and Media in 1991. The coalition argues that people would not tolerate other racial groups being used as mascots—with, say, fans wearing hokey Afros and calling their team the Negroes. Yet use of terms like *redskins* and fans making a mockery of traditional native dress are deemed acceptable by many Americans. AIM's education

Ojibwe in the Military

Ojibwe people have fought in every American war from the Revolution to Afghanistan. And Indians have served in the U.S. armed forces in larger numbers on a per capita basis than any other racial group in every American conflict since World War I, before they were even U.S. citizens. Many Anishinaabe enlisted for financial reasons. Poverty has been and remains prevalent in all of Minnesota's Ojibwe communities. The service was a way to earn money, provide for one's family, and escape from despair on the reservations.

Many servicemen saw the military as a way of finding a place in their families' military histories. The Ojibwe have had a long, storied military tradition, and serving in the armed forces was a way for Ojibwe people to gain respect within their tribes. Returning service members, using the respected position of *ogichidaa* (warrior), could speak at ceremonies, carry eagle staffs and flags at powwows, and remind others of the proud warrior heritage of the Ojibwe.

Anishinaabe veterans are typically well aware that the flag they served under also persecuted Indians and many others throughout its history, but they serve the U.S. military with pride and passion. According to Gulf War veteran and Mille Lacs tribal member Sean Fahrlander, "I said that if I have to protect white people in order to protect my people, I'll do it. Don't ever forget—this *land* is still my country."[ix]

World War I victory celebration. Elders in the photo are probably hereditary chiefs and veterans of tribal warfare and the U.S. Civil War. The young men in uniform are World War I veterans. All feathers were earned in battle unless part of a chief's bonnet.

and advocacy efforts have succeeded in convincing many schools to change their mascots, but it is an ongoing battle that meets with much resistance.

Fighting Dysfunction

In discussing the problems that Ojibwe communities face, many journalists, historians, and politicians have lost sight of the wonderful things about Indian country—resilient, surviving language and culture, authentic spiritual connection, a sense of community, sovereign power, and survival. Although there are many troubling chapters in Ojibwe history, what is most amazing is not what the Ojibwe have lost but what they have retained. That said, there are many problems in Ojibwe country, and they deserve an honest exploration. Painful and difficult though the discussion may be, problems can only be resolved when they are identified and faced head on. Among the most prevalent problems facing the Ojibwe today are high rates of drug and alcohol abuse, gangs, crime, chronic diseases (like diabetes), and poverty.

Poverty is at the heart of much of the dysfunction, and it is a long-standing problem. For the Ojibwe in Minnesota, the unemployment rate has been significantly high since the first reservation was created in the state. In 2000, unemployment remained at more than 20 percent in Minnesota's Ojibwe communities, compared to the state unemployment rate of 4.1 percent. More than 30 percent of the Ojibwe population lived below the poverty line, while only 5.1 percent of the state's overall population lived in poverty. Almost 60 percent of Indian households in Minnesota earned less than $35,000 in 2000, more than twice the rate for non-Indian households. The median tribal income was $28,533 that year, compared to $47,111 for white households.[48]

Poverty brings many problems with it. Drug and alcohol abuse and gangs pervade all poor population subsets

dysfunction ⇒ poverty

Tract 33, Cass Lake. Approximately 20 percent of the houses in this part of town were boarded up in September 2009, some abandoned, some uninhabitable, some vandalized. The Leech Lake tribal office, Head Start, housing, and court administration buildings are all within three blocks of this neighborhood.

in America, but this trouble is especially pronounced in Indian communities. Historical trauma from experiences in residential boarding schools, from assimilation policies, and from the destruction of tribal economies, landholdings, governments, and culture have added to despair and dysfunction. Indian minors are twice as likely as the general population to have consumed alcohol before age twelve, attempted suicide, or been sexually abused. Most years, there are more murders per capita in the Leech Lake Reservation town of Cass Lake (population 1,000) than in the Twin Cities metro area (population 2 million). In 2005, a horrific school shooting on the Red Lake Reservation brought national attention to the community but did not lead to a deeper understanding of the overarching crisis facing Minnesota's Ojibwe communities or bring additional resources to aid in efforts to fight the underlying problems.[49]

Education has the potential to help alleviate poverty and provide opportunities for tribal members. But the traumatic history of residential boarding schools, mission schools, and day schools contributes to community distrust of educational institutions. Pervasive substance abuse, violence, and peer pressure combine with this distrust to keep school dropout rates high. In Hennepin County, the dropout rate is 2 percent for the white population but 24 percent for the Indian population. Many students come to school exhausted because they are not properly monitored and rested or because there was a party at their house the night before. All they can do is sleep in class. Exposure to gangs at schools is also a problem. In Minnesota, 16 percent of sixth graders in the general population report that gang activity is a problem at their schools, but 32 percent of the sixth graders in the native population make the same report.[50]

dropout rate 24%

Education itself is stifled for many Ojibwe youth, no matter how bright and deserving they are. The lack of Ojibwe role models is being remedied, but slowly. Red Lake and Cass Lake school systems have more than 90 percent native students but very few native administrators, teachers, or support staff. The school districts cannot find many qualified Ojibwe to apply for open positions. Without Ojibwe staff who can establish role model rapport with the students and encourage them to continue their education, the vicious cycle continues. Although there are many inspiring examples of native and nonnative staff making breakthroughs with their pupils, and while Ojibwe students are graduating and going on to do amazing things, education and career advancement have come very slowly to the Ojibwe.

Being Ojibwe is hard. In addition to navigating a labyrinth of substance abuse and violence in their communities, Ojibwe people have few healthy outlets for solving many of their problems. Government programs are often inaccessible or unfair to many Indian people. The Indian Health Service (IHS), which is funded and run by the U.S. government, is the sole source of health care for many Indians. In the 1960s and 1970s, the IHS routinely sterilized

Indian women without their consent by tubal ligation, performing as many as twenty-five thousand such operations by 1975, according to one report. County, state, and federal programs do not always give Indians a fair shake. And some tribal programs have been plagued with accusations of mismanagement.[51]

As bad as dysfunction is, the problem may be made worse by anti-Indian bias. Many Minnesota Ojibwe feel that the state's justice system is racially biased against Indians. Indians comprise only 1.1 percent of the state population but 17 percent of the state's prison population. Yet Indians are not seventeen times more likely to commit crimes than people of other ethnic groups. The system disproportionally charges, convicts, and incarcerates Indians relative to the rate of Indian crime. Several studies have drawn troubling conclusions about racial profiling of Indians in Beltrami County and elsewhere in the state. Local and state agencies and task forces are investigating these trends.[52]

Enrolled Membership

who counts? Further complicating Ojibwe life is a highly contested debate over what it means to be Ojibwe. Tribal governments keep lists of enrolled members, or tribal citizens. Currently, more than fifty thousand Ojibwe people are enrolled tribal members in Minnesota but more than one hundred thousand people in the state identify themselves as Ojibwe.[53]

The problem is that to be an enrolled member of a Minnesota Chippewa Tribe reservation (any Minnesota Ojibwe reservation other than Red Lake), prospective members must document their Ojibwe ancestry, proving that they have at least 25 percent MCT Indian blood. Red Lake enrollees must prove that they have at least 25 percent Red Lake blood. Fathers who are not on birth certificates or don't sign voluntary recognition of paternity papers do not have their blood counted. Canadian Indians and members of other tribes who marry Minnesota Ojibwe tribal members do not have their blood counted.

Tribal records relating to ancestry are fraught with historical errors and miscalculations. Records at White Earth, for example, were compiled by eugenics-trained scientists Albert Jenks and Ales Hrdlicka, who scratched enrollees and noted any pink marks as evidence of nonnative blood. They also measured craniums and took hair samples. While such practices are now viewed as racist, records compiled by Jenks and Hrdlicka still comprise the database for determining tribal enrollment at White Earth today. As a result of this arcane system, there are many full-blooded Ojibwe from White Earth and other reservations in the state who cannot qualify to become enrolled members.[54]

While the Ojibwe population in Minnesota is growing very rapidly, the enrolled population is static or on the verge of declining on some reservations. White Earth and other tribes have tried to pass constitutional reforms that would change the criteria for enrollment, but the Minnesota Chippewa Tribe and the Bureau of Indian Affairs have stalled those efforts at every turn. It is a tremendous source of frustration for many Minnesota Ojibwe who want to belong, vote, and serve their tribes and people as bona fide members but cannot. The net result is that more than half of Minnesota's self-identified Ojibwe people suffer the drawbacks of their pernicious history and current community problems but enjoy none of the benefits of tribal membership.

Many Ojibwe people believe that if tribes are ever going to be effective in attacking the root of the problems that plague their communities, they must open the doors to tribal membership for all their people. Unfortunately, the advent of casino gaming and per capita payments in some place may actually slow the process. Some fear that expanding tribal membership criteria would lessen the benefits of tribal gaming—such as per capita payments and casino jobs—enjoyed by current members. The economic and political climate on the reservations is inherently divisive just when it needs to be inclusive, and the debate about identity fuels the bad feelings and paralysis that have plagued tribes for decades.[55]

Defining Tradition

Although programs that support education, job and career training, and employment are urgently needed in Ojibwe communities today, much community education needs to happen in both native and nonnative communities. Many Ojibwe people have internalized negative stereotypes about themselves. At powwows and casino restaurants "traditional fry-bread tacos" proliferate, yet fry bread is not traditional. It is an innovation that Ojibwe people developed out of necessity when they received rations of lard and flour from the U.S. government. Traditional food is wild rice, fish, berries, and wild game. Many native people laugh when confronted with the irony, but that misconception about traditional food is a killer: Native Americans have the highest rate of diabetes of any ethnic group in the world.

What is tradition

Babe's fry-bread stand at White Earth, 1998

In a similar vein, many Ojibwe have internalized the negative stereotype of the "lazy Indian." Jokes proliferate about "Indian time," and they echo a sad reality that is in fact the opposite of historical Ojibwe experience. Ojibwe people were extremely hardworking and physically fit as a necessary means of survival. The sedentary lifestyle of early reservation life has been internalized and now lauded by many Ojibwe people to their own detriment. Lazy is not Indian, though some people seem to think it is.

Similarly, many native people have taken on colonial misconceptions about poverty. Ojibwe people laugh about Indian cars (old, worn-out, held together by duct tape and baling wire), but there is nothing Indian about poverty. Poverty is an experience that all Ojibwe communities in Minnesota have endured, but it is not a defining feature of Ojibwe identity. Nevertheless, many Ojibwe have internalized such ideas, even sneering at and ridiculing those who have found gainful employment or gone to school. Traditional Ojibwe, who used to wear bandolier bags, vests, and the best clothes that their limited resources could afford for Midewiwin or Big Drum ceremonies, now regularly "dress down" for those events in jeans and T-shirts. Highly visible attributes of Ojibwe material culture are often missing from modern ceremonial functions as a result of Ojibwe misconceptions that demonstrations of poverty show or resonate with authentic Indianness. Ojibwe people need to think very carefully about how they think, write, and speak. Such misconceptions among the general population—which are even more pervasive—hold the Ojibwe back as well.[56]

The issues of substance abuse, violence, identity, and poverty are on the radar screen for many tribal officials, social workers, and educators. Vicious cycles of abuse and poverty can be successfully addressed. Yet the most powerful weapons for tackling those issues are, ironically, the ones closest to home, in the language and culture of the Ojibwe people.

Revitalizing Language and Culture

Language and culture Loss

Language and culture loss is one of the biggest concerns in Ojibwe country today. There are fewer than one thousand Ojibwe speakers in the United States, and nearly all of them reside in Minnesota. The statistics in the following sidebar are estimates and include community members displaced or living outside of their original communities. There are fewer than one hundred fluent Ojibwe speakers in Michigan, Wisconsin, and North Dakota combined. There are thousands more speakers of Ojibwe in Canada. However, even there, language loss is becoming readily apparent in many communities. Nancy Jones (Nigigoonsiminikaaning First Nation) estimates that there are twelve fluent speakers in her home community and perhaps six at Koochiching First Nation. These numbers indicate the difficulties the Ojibwe face in preserving traditional language and culture. Even within reservations, Ojibwe speakers tend to be concentrated. Almost all of the fluent speakers from Red Lake, for example, are from the community of Ponemah.[57]

Culture loss goes hand in hand with language loss. Traditional Ojibwe funerals are conducted exclusively in the Ojibwe language because it is believed that that language is what one's soul understands even if the person never spoke Ojibwe while alive. A small handful of qualified, fluent Ojibwe spiritual leaders now conduct all of the traditional funerals throughout the region. In the past, many people used to do this work in each Ojibwe community. Language is a critical tool for performing other ceremonies, too, ranging from naming ceremonies to traditional drums to initiations into the Midewiwin, the primary religious society of the Ojibwe. The language also contains the unique and irreplaceable Ojibwe worldview.[58]

Fluent Ojibwe Speakers in Minnesota[xi]	
Red Lake	400
Mille Lacs	150
Leech Lake	90
Bois Forte	20
White Earth	15
Grand Portage	3
Fond du Lac	0

Language is a critical attribute of sovereignty as well. After all, France is a nation because it has a land that is France and a language that is French. A Frenchman can be French even when he is traveling in China because of his language, culture, and homeland. It is the same for Ojibwe.

The growing assimilation of the Ojibwe population has come with a heavy price. As more tribal members move off the reservations for employment and education, watch television, play video games, form mixed-race marriages, and integrate into American society, they slowly step away from many aspects of Ojibwe culture. Fewer people harvest wild rice, make maple sugar, play moccasin games, make birch-bark canoes, and trap. Cultural loss is not limited to religious ceremonies and funerals but extends to the very fabric of daily life. Older traditional lifeways are fading, and the Ojibwe people are changing and evolving.

In spite of these losses, new forms of culture are growing. The modern powwow is ever present, vibrant, and accessible. Most Ojibwe in Minnesota attend powwows. Thousands have mastered the art of modern powwow dancing,

powwow

Jim Northrup III and his daughter Jaelisa Northrup harvesting wild rice, Perch Lake (Fond du Lac Reservation), 2003

Traditional Ojibwe crafts persist. Earl Otchingwanigan (Nyholm) bends cedar ribs for a birch-bark canoe, August 1997.

Earl Otchingwanigan (Nyholm) and Mark Wabamikee building a birch-bark canoe, August 1997

and the singing talent of Ojibwe youth is beyond question. Powwow is new and is influenced by many different tribal customs and even non-Indian events such as rodeos. The modern powwow is a healthy social event. But it is not a substitution for traditional Ojibwe religion or lifeways.

3 Evolved powwow

Tribes have to make some hard choices in the coming years if they want to reverse assimilation and continue to nourish the Ojibwe language and both old and new forms of culture. Currently, the money tribes devote to powwows completely overshadows the money they allocate to preserving and revitalizing the Ojibwe language. White Earth, for example, makes substantial monetary donations to Christian churches every year but typically fails to provide assistance when elders from Mille Lacs visit to advise and teach members of White Earth's ceremonial drums. By failing to adequately support Ojibwe language and traditional culture but offering overwhelming support to white religious institutions (like the churches) and new cultural

Dancers at Leech Lake Contest Powwow in Cass Lake, 2009

Nathan King Sr. and Nathan King Jr. singing with Northern Wind Singers at Leech Lake Contest Powwow, Cass Lake, 2009

forms (like the powwow) over old ones, tribal governments are accelerating cultural change.

Hope remains that the Ojibwe in Minnesota will preserve and revitalize their language and culture. The Maori of New Zealand, for instance, went from 7 percent fluency to 100 percent for all students in their school system and made Maoritanga one of the country's official languages. Native Hawaiians went from five hundred speakers to fifteen thousand. Both groups have enjoyed not only a revitalization of their traditional languages and cultures but also a major boost to community cohesion, pride, and solidarity. They've also seen the first meaningful declines in gang activity and drug and alcohol abuse in their histories. The Ojibwe could pursue the same goals in Minnesota.[59]

There is a growing desire among the Minnesota Ojibwe to stabilize and revitalize the Ojibwe language and culture. Hoping to do what the Maori and Native Hawaiians have done for their languages, three Ojibwe-language immersion schools have been operating for several years to share the language with young Ojibwe people in a total immersion environment. Those schools are Waadookodaading Ojibwe Immersion Charter School in Reserve, Wisconsin,

Niigaane Ojibwemowin Immersion School (housed within the Leech Lake Bug-O-Nay-Ge-Shig School) in Bena, Minnesota, and Wicoie Nandagikendan Early Childhood Immersion Project in Minneapolis. Mille Lacs helped develop new schools in 2008 at Lake Lena and East Lake, each with a significant focus on Ojibwe language and culture.

Education efforts to preserve language

Colleges and community education centers have also developed programs in hopes of building up people and resources for language and culture revitalization. Bemidji State University launched the first college Ojibwe language program in the state in 1968 and the first (and still only) academic journal of the Ojibwe language, the *Oshkaabewis Native Journal.* New dictionaries and bilingual and monolingual Ojibwe books are being published. The College of St. Scholastica, Bemidji State University, and Fond du Lac Tribal and Community College have been developing programs for training future generations of Ojibwe teachers. In 2009, community organizations in Bemidji successfully convinced many local businesses to write most of their signs bilingually in English and Ojibwe—for everything from bathrooms to produce.[60]

Niigaane Ojibwe Immersion Charter School

Niigaane Ojibwe Immersion Charter School was developed in 2003 to revitalize the Ojibwe language on the Leech Lake Reservation. It began with Adrian Liberty and others, who hoped to build the program out one year at a time, starting with the youngest students at the tribal Bug-O-Nay-Ge-Shig School and making the immersion program a school within a school. The idea was not to focus on teaching Ojibwe but rather to use the language as the medium of instruction in all subjects.

The immersion school's success was enabled by a clever reallocation of existing personnel and resources. Tribal elder and fluent speaker Mark Wakonabo, who had served for decades as janitor at the school, used his talent to teach alongside Liberty in the immersion school. Several other elders and community members volunteered their time to help teach the children. As tribal and grant support trickled in, more paid positions were created. The staff was challenged by a lack of published resources as they scrambled to write lesson plans, develop curriculum, and administer the program, sometimes staying only days ahead of the students' progress. Their hard work has yielded the intended result: the language naturally rolls off students' tongues, and recognition of and support for the school continue to grow.

Ojibwe Author Louise Erdrich

Louise Erdrich is among the most accomplished of Ojibwe writers. Her trilogy *Love Medicine, The Beet Queen,* and *Tracks* won the hearts of many readers and much critical acclaim, including the National Book Critics Circle Award. Her most recent work, *The Plague of Doves,* was a finalist for the Pulitzer Prize. She is also owner and operator of Birchbark Books, a small independent bookstore in Minneapolis.

The Ojibwe have also produced more writers than any other tribe in the country. Their ranks include Louise Erdrich, Gerald Vizenor, Kimberly Blaeser, Winona LaDuke, Jim Northrup, David Treuer, Brenda Child, Jean O'Brien, William Warren, George Copway, Walter Bresette, Maude Kegg, James Clark, Melvin Eagle, Archie Mosay, Thomas Peacock, Basil Johnston, and more. And most have done work that uses and supports the Ojibwe language.

Significant efforts at cultural revitalization are under way as well. Mille Lacs and other tribes have made meaningful investments in facilities for their ceremonies and programs for the Ojibwe language, including elaborate dance halls for their ceremonial drums, community centers for funerals, and a large, modern, year-round language immersion camp. White Earth tribal members have revitalized ceremonial drum culture on the reservation through repatriation of drums and a devotion to education in drum music, formal drum speeches, and ceremonial protocol from their cousins at Mille Lacs.

The Ojibwe can succeed in revitalizing their language and culture, but they need help. They need more Ojibwe people willing to learn, teach, and advocate for their language. More people must be willing to devote themselves to traditional lifeways and language. The Anishinaabe also need help from the outside. They need political support for sovereignty and program development. They need expertise and assistance in the creation and development of educational institutions, especially those that focus on language and culture. And they need money to fund the efforts already under way. Contrary to popular assumptions, most tribes and most tribal members are not well-off. There is plenty of work to do for anyone who cares, regardless of one's race. At stake is not just the linguistic and cultural heritage of the Ojibwe but the best chance the Ojibwe have to improve basic health and welfare for their people.

The state and the nation cannot repeat the terrible mistakes made in their previous treatment of the Minnesota Ojibwe, nor can they sit idly by while the battle for linguistic and cultural survival rages on. There is a part for all to play. History is not simply read; it is made.

Personal Account:
Reflections by Margaret Treuer

When I was growing up in the 1950s, nobody had jobs. We had to kill rabbits, partridge, and deer. And we had to poach a lot of our deer because the tribe didn't have a tribal hunting season. The tribe got our hunting rights affirmed in the 1970s. Before that, we were on our own. And wild rice. We really ate a lot of rice. I remember asking my mom why I always had to have rice for breakfast instead of corn flakes. But that's all we had. I can't remember a single fat Indian kid when I was growing up. We were outside all the time and we ate differently than now. And the DNR [Department of Natural Resources] was really after Indians in those days. When I was twelve I went ricing all day at Raven's Point with my friend Dina Stangel, who was only eleven. We had to. There were adults there too in other canoes, but we poled and knocked all of our own rice. There was a bad storm and we had a miserable time getting off the lake. The

Margaret Treuer, 2009

DNR was waiting right there. They took everyone's rice, ours included, and gave everyone tickets and fines.

My mom went to boarding school, and she raised us Catholic. One time my dad spent our family's last thirty-five cents on a plaque that read "The Lord Shall Provide." But we were so poor and my mom was so mad that she dished up the entire supper to us kids and put that plaque on my dad's plate for supper. We were poor, but the thing that really got us through the tough times was that the entire community helped each other. If you got a fifty-pound sack of flour, you dished it out to your neighbors and they did the same for you. And the community always came together for basketball games and Little League. That's all changed now.

My parents were really strict. I wasn't allowed to date in high school. One boy knew that, so he asked my dad if he could take me to a movie. My dad just said, "No. Hell, no." And that was the end of that.

I went to high school in Cass Lake and throughout my entire childhood I only remember one professional Indian ever. Her name was Corrine "Tiny" Kirt, and she was the school nurse. I spent a lot of my extra time in the nurse's office because it was the only place that felt comfortable to me in the entire school. That's why I decided I wanted to become a nurse and went to school at St. Luke's Nursing School in Duluth. I worked as a nurse in St. Cloud for a year and a half and then I came home to run the tribe's health program. I was the only Indian with a nursing degree who applied. I got married shortly after that, and we moved to Washington, DC, because of my husband's job.

In 1973, I volunteered to help Ada Deer and Sylvia Wilbur with the legislative efforts of the Menominee Indians. Their tribe had been terminated and the fight was on to have them reinstated. I helped write testimony, got letters of support from various organizations such as the League of Women Voters and the ACLU. By the time the bill for reinstatement of the Menominee came to a vote, there was only one dissenting vote. I was so excited about sovereignty, tribal rights, and the law that I applied to Catholic University Law School after that. I became the first Indian woman in the state of Minnesota with a law degree. We went home soon after that, and I started a private practice and then became a tribal judge, as I still am today.

I was raised as a Catholic, but it never stuck because it was never meant to be. I remember being sent to church as a child. There was an old man in Bena named George Martin. He got paid to caretake the church, turning on the heat and stuff like that. But he wasn't Catholic, not even close. He was Grand Medicine. He used to wear a little brown suit and stand in the back of that church, never sitting, just standing, and staring at me. As soon as he did that, I felt sick and had to leave the church. Time after time. I just made excuses to my parents why I couldn't stay. The priest tried to fondle me once, too, so I never liked it there. I used to lie awake at night and hear George Martin drumming in his house across town. That drum was calling me, and I always remember the way it sounded, drumming late into the night.

But my real spiritual awakening came as an adult. I did some legal work for Geraldine Smith, and she invited me to a pipe ceremony. I met Margaret Porter and Marian Medicine there. They took me to my first sweat with Frank Dickinson. Later I met Adam Lussier, and he doctored me a few times. Gerri took me to see Mary Roberts. She was so warm, inviting, and inclusive. I went fasting and eventually joined the lodge, with her guiding me along the way.

I have four amazing children. People sometimes ask me how I raised four kids who are all so smart, accomplished, and together. I don't know how to answer that. I never dreamed growing up that I would spawn writers, professors, doctors, and lawyers, much less that I would become a lawyer. I sheltered them as much as I could from exposure to drinking, drugs, and violence. I emphasized education, but not just from books. I took care to teach them traditional ways, how to pick rice, finish and cook it, how to make maple syrup, preserve blueberries, how to snare rabbits, hunt deer, and garden. I tried to show them who they were by connecting them to the healthy parts of being Indian by taking them to ceremonies. Nothing can stop an Indian who knows who he is.

Suggestions for Further Reading

Ojibwe Language and Culture

Kegg, Maude. *Portage Lake: Memories of an Ojibwe Childhood.* Minneapolis: University of Minnesota Press, 1991.

Moose, Lawrence L., et al. *Aaniin Ekidong: Ojibwe Vocabulary Project.* St. Paul: Minnesota Humanities Center, 2009.

Nichols, John D., and Earl Nyholm (Otchingwanigan). *A Concise Dictionary of Minnesota Ojibwe.* Minneapolis: University of Minnesota Press, 1995.

Treuer, Anton. *Living Our Language: Ojibwe Tales and Oral Histories.* St. Paul: Minnesota Historical Society Press, 2001.

Early Ojibwe History

Copway, George. *The Traditional History and Characteristic Sketches of the Ojibway Nation.* London: Charles Gilpin, 1850.

Tanner, Helen Hornbeck, ed. *Atlas of Great Lakes Indian History.* Norman: University of Oklahoma Press, 1987.

Warren, William W. *History of the Ojibway People.* 1885. Reprint, St. Paul: Minnesota Historical Society Press, 1984.

Legal History

Duthu, N. Bruce. *American Indians and the Law.* London: Penguin Books, 2008.

Getches, David H., and Charles F. Wilkinson. *Federal Indian Law: Cases and Materials.* St. Paul, MN: West Publishing, 1986.

Contemporary Minnesota Ojibwe History and Government
Indian Policy

Adams, David Wallace. *Education for Extinction: American Indians and the Boarding School Experience, 1875–1928*. Lawrence: University Press of Kansas, 1995.

Child, Brenda. *Boarding School Seasons: American Indian Families, 1900–1940*. Lincoln: University of Nebraska Press, 1998.

Graves, Kathy David, and Elizabeth Ebbott. *Indians in Minnesota*. Minneapolis: University of Minnesota Press, 2006.

Hoxie, Frederick. *A Final Promise: The Campaign to Assimilate the Indians, 1880–1920*. New York: Routledge, 2001.

Olson, James, and Raymond Wilson. *Native Americans in the Twentieth Century*. Urbana: University of Illinois Press, 1986.

Notes

1. There are a few scattered references to "powwow" as old as the late nineteenth century, but they are actually references to ceremonial Big Drum dances, rather than powwows as they are performed and understood today. Modern powwow culture first emerged around World War II, and its current contest configurations developed in the 1970s.

2. Ojibwe emergence as a distinct people is derived from linguistic analysis, archaeological evidence, and oral history. See William Warren, *History of the Ojibway People* (St. Paul: Minnesota Historical Society Press [hereafter, MHS Press], 1984); George Copway, *The Traditional History and Characteristic Sketches of the Ojibway Nation* (London: Charles Gilpin, 1850); Johann Georg Kohl, *Kitchi-Gami: Life among the Lake Superior Ojibway* (St. Paul: MHS Press, 1985). Information on the evolution of the Ojibwe language, dialect variance, and its relationship to other Algonquian languages is based on Anton Treuer, *Living Our Language: Ojibwe Tales & Oral Histories* (St. Paul: MHS Press, 2001); John D. Nichols and Earl Nyholm, *A Concise Dictionary of Minnesota Ojibwe* (Minneapolis: University of Minnesota Press, 1995); J. Randolph Valentine, *Nishnaabemwin Reference Grammar* (Toronto: University of Toronto Press, 2001).

3. For further reading on the meaning of the term *Ojibwe,* see Theresa M. Schenck, *The Voice of the Crane Echoes Afar: The Sociopolitical Organization of the Lake Superior Ojibwa, 1640–1855* (New York: Garland, 1997), 22; Warren, *History of the Ojibway People,* 36–37; George

Copway, *Traditional History,* 30. *Bwaa* is the correct double-vowel orthography equivalent to *bwa,* as it appears in the Warren orthography. The morphological components of *ozhibii'ige* ("he writes") are known to everyday speakers of Ojibwe. However, this word is similarly glossed in Nichols and Nyholm, *Concise Dictionary.*

4. The Ojibwe clan system is well documented in oral histories and anthropological sketches of the Ojibwe. See especially, Warren, *History of the Ojibway People;* Copway, *Traditional History.* Also based on interviews: Archie Mosay, 1992; Thomas J. Stillday, 1995; Anna Gibbs, 1995; James Clark, 1994.

Intraclan marriage was the only internal domestic action punishable by death. Rarely, cases of murder were avenged, but as a matter of consistent tribal custom, this taboo was the strongest. Warfare and other intertribal altercations had their own rules. Edward Benton-Banai, *The Mishomis Book: The Voice of the Ojibway* (Hayward, WI: Indian Country Communications, 1988), 74–78; Warren, *History of the Ojibway People,* 50–52.

5. Benton-Banai, *Mishomis Book,* 74–78; Warren, *History of the Ojibway People,* 50–52. The selection of chiefs by election rather than hereditary right in newly settled areas is well attested in primary source documents. See especially Copway, *Traditional History,* 140. See also Mentor L. Williams, *Schoolcraft's Narrative Journal of Travels* (East Lansing: Michigan State University Press, [1951] 1992), 486. There are now more than twenty clans represented at Red Lake. The tribal flag still

only displays the original clans that settled there. Interview, Eugene Stillday, 2009.

6. Ojibwe people universally attest to the great respect given to elders in their culture, an attitude that is also built right into the language. The Ojibwe word for old woman, *mindimooye*, literally means "one who holds things together," describing the role of the family matriarch. The word for old man, *akiwenzii*, literally means "earth caretaker." The basic words for elder, *gichi-anishinaabe* and *gichi-aya'aa*, literally mean "great being." For a great theoretical discussion of age in Ojibwe culture, see Michael D. McNally, *Honoring Elders: Aging, Authority, and Ojibwe Religion* (New York: Columbia University Press, 2009).

7. Thomas Vennum Jr., *Wild Rice and the Ojibway People* (St. Paul: MHS Press, 1988); Benton-Banai, *Mishomis Book*.

8. Charles C. Mann, *1491: New Revelations of the Americas before Columbus* (New York: Knopf, 2005); Alvin Josephy Jr., *500 Nations: An Illustrated History of North American Indians* (New York: Alfred A. Knopf, 1994); Jack Leustig, *500 Nations*, video documentary (Los Angeles: Warner Home Video, 1995). Reuben Gold Thwaites, ed., *The Jesuit Relations and Allied Documents*, 73 vols. (New York: Pageant Book Company, 1959).

9. Calvin Martin, *Keepers of the Game: Indian-Animal Relationships and the Fur Trade* (Los Angeles: University of California Press, 1982).

10. This dynamic is especially well reported in Richard White, *The Middle Ground: Indians, Empires and Republics in the Great Lakes Region, 1650–1815* (Cambridge, UK: Cambridge University Press, 1991). Virgil J. Vogel, *Indian Names in Michigan* (Ann Arbor: University of Michigan Press, 1986); Charles L. Cutler, *O Brave New Words: Native American Loanwords in Current English* (Norman: University of Oklahoma Press, 1992); Warren Upham, *Minnesota Geographic Names*, 3rd ed. (St. Paul: Minnesota Historical Society Press, 2001). Sylvia Van Kirk, *Many Tender Ties: Women in Fur-Trade Society* (Norman: University of Oklahoma Press, 1980). Tribal Membership Roll, Minnesota Chippewa Tribe. There are also many people with the last name *French* (spelled in English), and the last name *English* or a corruption of the Ojibwe word for Englishman, "Auginaush."

11. Helen Hornbeck Tanner, ed., *Atlas of Great Lakes Indian History* (Norman: University of Oklahoma Press, 1987); White, *The Middle Ground*.

12. Grand Portage Chairman John B. Flatte presented the British medals to the Minnesota Historical Society in 1970.

13. Information on Ojibwe people seeking refuge from the Iroquois Wars with the Dakota, the Ojibwe-Dakota peace conference at Fond du Lac, and the eruption of hostilities between the Ojibwe and the Dakota is taken from Thwaites, *Jesuit Relations*, 5:290, 55:97; Tanner, *Atlas*, 29–35, 42–43; Warren, *History of the Ojibway People*, 155–326; Lawrence J. Burpee, *Journals and Letters of Pierre Gaultier de Varennes de La Vérendrye and His Sons* (Toronto, ON: The Champlain Society, 1968); Emma Helen Blair, *The Indian Tribes of the Upper Mississippi Valley and Region of the Great Lakes as Described by Nicolas Perrot*, 2 vols. (Cleveland, OH: Arthur H. Clark, 1912), 160–63; Louise Phelps Kellogg, *The British Regime in Wisconsin and the Old Northwest* (Madison: State Historical Society of Wisconsin, 1935); Louise Phelps Kellogg, *Early Narratives of the*

Northwest, 1634–1699 (New York: Charles Scribner's Sons, 1917); Louise Phelps Kellogg, *The French Regime in Wisconsin and the Northwest* (Madison: State Historical Society of Wisconsin, 1925), 95, 99, 153–54; William W. Folwell, *A History of Minnesota*, 4 vols. (St. Paul: MHS Press, 1956), 1: 80. There were also large numbers of Ottawa Indians in attendance at this event.

14. Tanner, *Atlas*, 65.

15. Samuel Pond, *The Dakota or Sioux in Minnesota* (St. Paul: MHS Press, 1986), 86–99, 110–11, 159–61. Pond insists that the Dakota Wakan Dance was not Dakota in origin (92). Interviewee Archie Mosay claims it was a gift to the Dakota from the Ojibwe. The Sun Dance eventually replaced the Wakan Dance as the primary ceremony of the Sioux. Sun Dance, however, is a plains ceremony that the Sioux acquired only as they moved west many years later. It was never practiced in Minnesota until the twentieth century. Now there are several Sun Dances held in southern Minnesota.

16. Details on Ojibwe-Dakota warfare are taken from Warren, *History of the Ojibway People;* Tanner, *Atlas;* Pond, *Dakota or Sioux;* Copway, *Traditional History;* Kohl, *Kitchi-Gami;* and Maude Kegg, "Nookomis Gaa-inaajimotawid," *Oshkaabewis Native Journal* 1.2 (1990).

17. Thomas Vennum, *The Ojibwa Dance Drum: Its History and Construction* (St. Paul: MHS Press, 2009).

18. Article 5 of the treaty reads, "The privilege of hunting, fishing, and gathering the wild rice, upon the lands, the rivers and the lakes included in the territory ceded, is guaranteed to the Indians." Charles J. Kappler, *Laws and Treaties*, 2 vols. (Washington, DC: GPO, 1904), 2:491–93. See also Tanner, *Atlas;* William W. Folwell, *A History of Minnesota*, 4 vols. (St. Paul: MHS Press, 1956); Rebecca Kugel, *To Be the Main Leaders of Our People: A History of Minnesota Ojibwe Politics* (East Lansing: Michigan State University Press, 1998); James M. McClurken, ed., *Fish in the Lakes, Wild Rice and Game in Abundance: Testimony on Behalf of the Mille Lacs Ojibwe Hunting and Fishing Rights* (East Lansing: Michigan State University Press, 2000).

19. Information on the Sandy Lake Annuity Fiasco is taken from Bagone-giizhig, letter to the editor, *Minnesota Democrat*, July 15, 1851; Bagone-giizhig, Open Letter to William W. Warren, *Minnesota Pioneer*, Jan. 16, 1851; William W. Warren, letter to the editor, *Minnesota Democrat*, Jan. 28, 1851; Sela Wright to J. Bardwell, Feb. 1, 1851, Manuscripts Relating to Northwest Missions, Grace Lee Nute Papers, MHS; *Minnesota Democrat*, Jan. 21 and Dec. 10, 1851; *Minnesota Pioneer*, Nov. 21, 1850; William W. Warren to George P. Warren, June 24, 1852, Charles Francis Xavier Goldsmith Papers, State Historical Society of Wisconsin, 1:4; William W. Warren to Alexander Ramsey, Jan. 21, 1851, enclosed with Ramsey to Luke Lea, Jan. 28, 1851, M1171, National Archives Microfilm Publications, M 234, R767, 133–34. John S. Watrous to Alexander Ramsey, Dec. 22, 1851, M203, R6; Alexander Ramsey diaries, vol. 21, Jan. 8–9, 1851, M203, R38; Flat Mouth Speech at Sandy Lake, Transcribed, Translated and Sent to Alexander Ramsey, Dec. 3, 1850, M203, R5, all in Alexander Ramsey Family Papers, MHS. Julia Warren Spears, "My Journey with the Chippewa Indians," written Sep. 1921, "Reminiscence of the Assassination of Hole-in-the-Day," "Reminiscences of a Short History of the Chippewa Chief Hole-in-the-Day," and

"Reminiscences of Hole-in-the-Day," all in Julia Warren Spears Papers, Minnesota Historical Society, 1.

20. The nature of government control of reservations through Indian agents, Indian police, and courts of Indian offenses is well attested in Frederick Hoxie, *The Campaign to Assimilate the Indians* (Lincoln: University of Nebraska Press, 2001); James Olson and Raymond Wilson, *Native Americans in the Twentieth Century* (Urbana: University of Illinois Press, 1986).

21. Olson and Wilson, *Native Americans*, 97.

22. Cited in David Wilkins, *American Indian Sovereignty and the U.S. Supreme Court: The Masking of Justice* (Austin: University of Texas Press, 1997), 36. The Indian residential boarding school system has been widely reported. See *Woodlands: The Story of the Mille Lacs Ojibwe,* oral history video documentary (Onamia, MN: Mille Lacs Band of Ojibwe, 1994); David Wallace Adams, *Education for Extinction: American Indians and the Boarding School Experience, 1875–1928* (Lawrence: University Press of Kansas, 1995); Tim Giago, *Children Left Behind: The Dark Legacy of Indian Mission Boarding Schools* (Santa Fe, NM: Clear Light Publishing, 2006); Colin Calloway, *First Peoples: A Documentary Survey of American Indian History* (Boston: Bedford/St. Martin's, 2004), 335–96.

23. Commissioner of Indian Affairs William A. Jones, speech to Congress, 1899. All statistics about the health conditions and death rates at the residential schools are taken from Lewis Merriam, *The Problem of Indian Administration: Report of a Survey Made at the Request of Honorable Hubert Work, Secretary of the Interior, and Submitted to Him, February 28, 1928* (Baltimore, MD: Johns Hopkins

University Press, 1928), better known as the Merriam Report.

24. Alexandra Pierce, "Shattered Hearts" (report compiled for Minnesota Indian Women's Resource Center, August 2009), 83.

25. Michael Krauss, "Status of Native American Language Endangerment," in Gina Cantoni, ed., *Stabilizing Indigenous Languages* (Flagstaff: Northern Arizona University, 1996), 17. Lawrence L. Moose, et al., *Aaniin Ekidong: Ojibwe Vocabulary Project* (St. Paul: Minnesota Humanities Center, 2009), 4.

26. "The Real Story of the Chippewa National Forest," *Minnesota Conservation Volunteer* (St. Paul: Minnesota Department of Natural Resources, Nov./Dec. 2004); Folwell, *History of Minnesota,* 4:254–61. National forests are managed very differently from national parks. The Chippewa National Forest and others like it are logged regularly, in strips, clear-cuts, and selected harvests. A beauty strip is maintained along Highway 2 and lakeshores for tourism.

27. For information about the Nelson Act of 1889, see Folwell, *History of Minnesota,* 4:219–35; *Chippewa Indians in Minnesota,* 51st Congress, 1st session, *House Executive Documents,* serial 2747 (Washington, DC: GPO), 247:1–12 (includes a full report from Henry Rice on flooding from dams, survey problems, and abortive legislation on arrearages and compensation), 822–27. For information on allotment in Minnesota, see Melissa Meyer, *The White Earth Tragedy: Ethnicity and Dispossession at a Minnesota Anishinaabe Reservation* (Lincoln: University of Nebraska Press, 1994), 51–52, 64–65; and Folwell, *History of Minnesota,* 4:265–68. For information on the Clapp Rider legislation and the

Steenerson Act, see *Congressional Record,* 56th Congress, 1st session, 56, 2566; *Congressional Record,* 58th Congress, 2nd session, 685, 3660, 4413, 5546, 5825; Commissioner of Indian Affairs, *Statutes at Large,* 33:539; Folwell, *History of Minnesota,* 4:266–67. House of Representatives, "Report in the Matter of the Investigation of the White Earth Reservation," 62nd Congress, 3rd session, Report Number 1336, serial 6336 (Washington, DC: GPO), submitted Jan. 16, 1913, 5 (Graham Report).

One elder I interviewed, Joseph Auginaush, showed me the $24 grocery receipt over which his father had lost their family's allotment by Roy Lake. The trader had allowed the family to charge food at his post and then presented his charge slip to the allotment officer and demanded title to the Auginaush allotment in lieu of payment for the groceries. The allotment officer promptly turned the title over to the trader. The Auginaush family was not consulted in the transaction, and there was no due process of law, no notice, no serving of papers, no hearing. When the family complained to the allotment officer, it was simply given the grocery receipt, which it still keeps as both evidence and a reminder of treachery. This is just one of many such mistreatments that occurred during the allotment process. The abuses at White Earth were among the worst.

28. Land claims at White Earth were especially complicated because of allotment and relocation occurring simultaneously. In 1986, the federal government passed the White Earth Land Settlement Act, which was intended to provide just financial compensation to allottees and their heirs and clear title on clouded allotment parcels. It also paid the White Earth tribal government $6.6 million for economic development, much of which directly supported or leveraged construction of the Shooting Star Casino. It has been a source of controversy for many people because the process is cumbersome, slow, and difficult for allottee heirs to navigate. It is further complicated by requirements that claims open for two years be paid to the tribe instead of allottees, which some people fear has excluded many eligible tribal members who did not respond for any number of reasons. Others are upset that the act legalizes all previous illegalities in land transfers over each parcel with no apologies and that compensation seems paltry when divided among numerous heirs. WELSA has been amended several times.

29. Olson and Wilson, *Native Americans;* Hoxie, *Campaign to Assimilate;* Kathy David Graves and Elizabeth Ebbott, *Indians in Minnesota* (Minneapolis: University of Minnesota Press, 2006), 16–18, 29–30, 57, 62, 165; Calloway, *First Peoples,* 400–436. All tribes that accepted reorganization disbanded their courts of Indian offenses and Indian police, reorganizing under the new structures of the IRA. Tribes that voted not to accept the IRA kept those structures but renamed and modified them. For all tribes, the BIA became advisory rather than supervisory. Tribal constitutions were boiler plates, based on a corporate governance model.

30. White Earth Tribal Chair Erma Vizenor in particular has asserted that White Earth is a sovereign nation and does not need approval from the BIA or the MCT for its constitutional reforms. However, constitutional reform without sanction from both organizations could jeopardize federal funding for tribal operations, crippling the ability of the tribe to maintain

services that tribal members have come to expect. It is difficult for any tribe to please its people without federal funding, but accepting federal help often impinges on self-determination. *Anishinaabeg Today: A Chronicle of the White Earth Band of Ojibwe* 11.17 (Dec. 13, 2006): 3.

31. Those reforms have passed at the tribal level but need approval from the MCT and the BIA to become effective, and that support is uncertain.

32. The status of tribal sovereignty and congressional plenary power over Indian affairs is widely reported. See N. Bruce Duthu, *American Indians and the Law* (London: Penguin Books, 2008); Charles F. Wilkinson, *American Indians, Time and the Law* (New Haven, CT: Yale University Press, 1987); David H. Getches and Charles F. Wilkinson, *Federal Indian Law: Cases and Materials* (St. Paul, MN: West Publishing, 1986).

33. Public Law 280, Act of Aug. 15, 1953, ch. 505, 67 Stat. 588; Kevin K. Washburn, "The Legacy of *Bryan v. Itasca County*: How an Erroneous $147 County Tax Notice Helped Bring Tribes $200 Billion in Indian Gaming Revenue," *Minnesota Law Review* 92.4 (April 2008): 919–70; and the Harvard Project on American Indian Economic Development, *The State of the Native Nations: Conditions under U.S. Policies of Self-Determination* (New York: Oxford University Press, 2008).

34. *Bryan v. Itasca County* (426 U.S. 373, 1976). In *State of Minnesota v. Stone* and *State of Minnesota v. Jackson,* the Minnesota Supreme Court ruled that the state could not regulate most traffic laws on reservations for Indian defendants.

35. Information on termination is derived from Washburn, "The Legacy of *Bryan v. Itasca County*"; Calloway, *First*

Peoples, 397–55; Hoxie, *Campaign to Assimilate.*

36. Information on the treaty rights disputes and court cases in Wisconsin and Minnesota is derived from Anton Treuer, "The Miner's Canary: An Analysis of the Ojibway Spearfishing Rights Dispute in Wisconsin" (senior thesis, Princeton University, 1991); Rick Whaley and Walt Bresette, *Walleye Warriors: The Chippewa Treaty Rights Story* (Warner, NH: Tongues of Green Fire Press, 1994); and McClurken, *Fish in the Lakes.* The Great Lakes Indian Fish and Wildlife Commission's quarterly publication, *Mazina'igan,* is devoted exclusively to documenting tribal natural resource harvest and management and all legal issues relevant to those endeavors.

37. All of the statistics on adoption and foster care of native children, including the Minnesota-specific figures, are taken from expert testimony on the bill, Public Law 95–608 (Indian Child Welfare Act), 9–10, 336–37.

38. Native American Graves Protection and Repatriation Act, Public Law 101–601, 104 Statute 3048 (Nov. 16, 1990).

39. Felix S. Cohen, *Felix S. Cohen's Handbook of Federal Indian Law* (Charlottesville, VA: Michie, 1982). Justice Hugo Black (1960), cited in Treuer, "Miner's Canary," 81.

40. Information on the legal, social, economic, and political dimensions of tribal gaming is derived from Graves and Ebbott, *Indians in Minnesota,* 129–58; Calloway, *First Peoples,* 484–95; *Bryan v. Itasca County* was especially significant because the decision clarified that Public Law 280 did not give states civil *regulatory* control over tribes.

41. *Seminole v. Butterworth,* 657 F.2d 310, U.S. Court of Appeals, Fifth Circuit.

42. Graves and Ebbott, *Indians in Minnesota*, 160–61.

43. Mille Lacs Band of Ojibwe website, http://www.millelacsojibwe.org. Graves and Ebbott, *Indians in Minnesota*, 160–61.

44. Indian Citizenship Act of 1924, 43 U.S. Statutes at Large, Chapter 233, 253. Jury duty is awarded to citizens based on a lottery of registered voters. Indian abstention from voting thus greatly reduces the chances of Indians receiving a trial by their peers.

45. Technically, the constitution of the Minnesota Chippewa Tribe requires that the executive committee, which is comprised of chairs from each member reservation, request a BIA election by referendum vote of MCT members. Some tribes have been very resistant to constitutional reforms that change blood quantum as the criterion for enrollment or allow other tribes to separate from MCT because either action could impact federal funding or per capita payments.

46. Red Lake Chairman Roger Jourdain led a boycott of Bemidji area businesses in 1967 in response to the remarks of Beltrami County Commissioner Robert Kohl, who went on a racial rant on the local radio station, KBUN. The boycott was joined by Leech Lake and White Earth. Together, the three tribes comprise about half the shopping population in Bemidji. Initially the Bemidji Area Chamber of Commerce tried to apologize on Kohl's behalf, but the boycott continued until Kohl himself apologized. Realizing the importance of his Ojibwe patrons, Joseph Lueken, owner of the local grocery chain, instituted an affirmative action employment policy after the boycott as well. Chuck Haga, "Red Lake: From Condemnation to Compassion During a Crisis," *Minneapolis Star Tribune*, available: http://www.rlnn.com/ArtMar06/RL FromCondemnationCompassionDuring Crisis.html. Information on AIM activism is taken from Paul Smith and Robert Warrior, *Like a Hurricane: The American Indian Movement from Alcatraz to Wounded Knee* (New York: W. W. Norton, 1996).

47. Information on these AIM activities is taken primarily from "Concerned Indian Americans," Charter Statement; Interview, Clyde Bellecourt, 1994; Russell Means, *Where White Men Fear to Tread* (New York: St. Martin's Press, 1995).

48. Graves and Ebbott, *Indians in Minnesota*, 160–61, 271.

49. Pierce, "Shattered Hearts," 64, 77, 87. See also pages 29 and 63 for a discussion of general maltreatment reports from native youth and higher rates of coercion into sex trafficking. Some of the murders themselves are exceptionally brutal. A blind man was beaten to death by teenagers in Cass Lake. Another teenager was killed by torture, having his tattoos removed with a blowtorch. The school shooting at Red Lake took place March 21, 2005, when sixteen-year-old Jeffrey Weise killed his grandfather and his grandfather's girlfriend and then drove to Red Lake high school, where he shot an unarmed security guard, five students, and a teacher before killing himself. See Jim Ragsdale, "Kindred Spirits: The Red Lake Shootings," *St. Paul Pioneer Press* (March 27, 2005), A1, A7; Jim Ragsdale, "In Mourning, Reservation and Nearby Bemidji Are Pulled Together," *Duluth News Tribune* (March 27, 2005), 7A; and "Red Lake Massacre," http://en.wikipedia.org/wiki/ Red_Lake_massacre.

50. Pierce, "Shattered Hearts," 48, 83.

51. Pierce, "Shattered Hearts," 11.

52. Graves and Ebbott, *Indians in Minnesota,* 92, 288.

53. Graves and Ebbott, *Indians in Minnesota,* 91.

54. Information on tribal enrollment at White Earth and the Jenks and Hrdlicka tests is taken from David L. Beaulieu, "Curly Hair and Big Feet: Physical Anthropology and the Implementation of Land Allotment on the White Earth Chippewa Reservation," *American Indian Quarterly* (Fall 1984): 281–314; Folwell, *History of Minnesota,* 4:291–93; Ales Hrdlicka, "Anthropology of the Chippewa," *Holmes Anniversary Volume: Anthropological Essays* (Washington, DC: privately printed, 1916), 198–227. White Earth is trying to change the criteria for enrollment, but absent approval from the BIA and the MCT, it has been unsuccessful to date.

55. It is a mutually beneficial proposition. More people would be eligible for help from the tribes, but expanding tribal membership would help the tribes by having larger pools of voters, tribal political leaders, advocates, and educators. Waning membership means waning political power. Italy and Japan, for example, have declined in military and diplomatic position in part because of declining birth rates relative to those of other countries.

56. One of the most authentic and approachable explorations of Indian identity is Thomas Vennum, *Just Too Much of an Indian: Bill Baker, Stalwart in a Fading Culture* (LaPointe, WI: Just Too Much of an Indian Press, 2008).

57. Moose et al., *Aaniin Ekidong,* 4; Anton Treuer, "The Importance of Language: A Closer Look," *Oshkaabewis Native Journal* 4.1 (Spring 1997): 3–11; Cantoni, *Stabilizing Indigenous Languages,* and Jon Reyhner, ed., *Teaching Indigenous Languages* (Flagstaff: Northern Arizona University, 1997).

58. Morphological components of the language are embedded with meaning. *Dewe'igan* (drum) literally means "heartbeat," which explains the physical and spiritual location of the ceremonial drum at the heart or center of the ceremony. Every other word is equally laden with value, perspective, and understanding. These meanings make Ojibwe thinking different from English thinking. Critical differences of the value and importance of age, gender, and relationships with the natural world abound in the language.

59. Leanne Hinton, *How to Keep Your Language Alive: A Commonsense Approach to One-on-One Language Learning* (Berkeley, CA: Heydey Books, 2002).

60. Fond du Lac Tribal and Community College is a model of cooperative governance. It is jointly funded by the Fond du Lac Reservation and the State of Minnesota but operated by an independent board of trustees.

Notes to Sidebars

i. The archaeological evidence challenging the Clovis First Theory (Bering Strait Theory) is broad and deep, widely published in many journals since the early 1970s. A sample of the major sources I consulted follow: James Adovasio and Jake Page, *The First Americans: In Pursuit of Archaeology's Greatest Mystery* (New York: Random House, 2003); N. Guidon and G. Delibrias, "Carbon-14 Dates Point to Man in the Americas 32,000 Years Ago," *Nature* 321 (1986): 769–71; Robson Bonnichsen and Karen L. Turnmire, *Clovis: Origins and Adaptations* (Corvallis: Oregon State University Press, 1991); Mary C. Stiner, "Modern Human Origins—Faunal

Perspectives," *Annual Review of Anthropology* (1993): 55–77; David Hurst Thomas, *Exploring Ancient Native America: An Archaeological Guide* (New York: Macmillan, 1994); David S. Whitley and Ronald I. Dorn, "New Perspectives on the Clovis vs. Pre-Clovis Controversy," *American Antiquity* 58.4 (1993): 626–47; John Noble Wilford, "Support for Early Date of Arrival in America," *New York Times,* Feb. 1, 1994; Mann, *1491.* Other sites under current excavation and investigation that challenge the Clovis First Theory include Channel Islands (California), Leech Lake (Walker, Minnesota), Big Eddy Site (Missouri), Page-Ladson (Jefferson County, Florida), Mud Lake and Schaefer-Hebior Mammoth Sites (Kenosha County, Wisconsin), Paisley Caves (Oregon), Cactus Hill (Virginia), Tlapacoya (Lake Chalco Pedra Furada, Serra da Capivara National Park, Brazil), Lagoa Santa (Minas Gerais, Brazil), and Cueva Fell and Pali Aike Crater (Patagonia), Taima Taima (Venezuela).

ii. The connections between these words and their Ojibwe counterparts are obvious to Ojibwe speakers. See also Nichols and Nyholm, *Concise Dictionary;* Vogel, *Indian Names in Michigan;* Cutler, *O Brave New Words;* Upham, *Minnesota Place Names.*

iii. The gendered division of labor in Ojibwe culture, the concept of balance as opposed to equality, and the role of homosexuality in Ojibwe society are well documented in oral histories and archival material. Interviews: Earl Otchingwanigan (Nyholm), 1992; Mary Roberts, 1988, 1989; Archie Mosay, 1993; Dora Ammann, 1994; Thomas J. Stillday, 1995; Anna Gibbs, 1998. Martha Coleman Bray, *The Journals of Joseph N. Nicollet: A Scientist on the Mississippi Headwaters with Notes on Indian Life, 1836–37,* trans. André Fertey (St.

Paul: MHS Press, 1970), 165, 199–211; Edwin James, ed., *A Narrative of the Captivity and Adventures of John Tanner during Thirty Years Residence among the Indians in the Interior of North America* (1830; repr., Minneapolis: Ross and Haines, 1956), 105–6; John Parker, ed., *The Journals of Jonathan Carver and Related Documents* (St. Paul: MHS Press, 1976), 108–10; Warren, *History of the Ojibway People,* 264; Kugel, *To Be the Main Leaders,* 71–73, 92n.

iv. Warren, *History of the Ojibway People,* 165; Interview, Vernon Whitefeather, 1997. The Dakota clan system that dominated their social fabric has now been thoroughly eroded and supplanted with a still vital kinship system embedded in their language and customs. However, historically the Dakota acquired the merman clan from Ojibwe paternity in mixed marriages at the same time that the Ojibwe acquired the wolf and kingfisher clans from the Dakota.

v. Information on the Battle of Sugar Point is taken from William E. Matsen, "Battle of Sugar Point: A Re-examination," *Minnesota History* (fall 1987): 269–75; Associated Press, "Emma Bear, Last Survivor of Battle of Sugar Point, Dead at 103," *Brainerd Daily Dispatch,* July 17, 2001. The arrest of Hole in the Day which sparked this event was actually his second. In the first case, he was brought to Duluth for trial and left on his own to return home. The battle was the last "Indian war," although some would say that the AIM takeover of the Wounded Knee Trading Post in South Dakota should also be termed a war, as it did involve U.S. military action and there were casualties.

vi. Information on termination, relocation, and Public Law 280 is derived from Washburn, "The Legacy of *Bryan v. Itasca*

County"; Calloway, *First Peoples*, 397–55; Hoxie, *Campaign to Assimilate*.

vii. Graves and Ebbott, *Indians in Minnesota*, 92, 95.

viii. Unemployment statistics in this section were taken from Graves and Ebbott, *Indians in Minnesota*, 160–61. Those figures are based on the year 2000 census data. There was a surge in unemployment rates for both Indians and the general population during the recession that began in 2008.

ix. Fahrlander placed the emphasis on *land* to clarify that he was serving his people and his place, not the U.S. flag. He also added, "Things were so bad on the reservation that what we were going to was no worse than what we were coming from."

x. Graves and Ebbott, *Indians in Minnesota*, 95. This data is for the enrolled tribal population. The number of self-identified Indians living on a reservation is much smaller.

xi. Moose, et al., *Aaniin Ekidong*, 4.

Index

Page numbers in *italic* refer to pictures and captions; page numbers such as '87n1' refer to notes, e.g., note 1 on page 87.

Tribal governments: citizenship and civil rights, 60; enrolled membership, 70–72; IRA and, 41–43, 91n29, 91n30; political conflicts, 62, 93n45; restrictions on tribal leadership, 30
Tribble, Fred, 49

Unemployment, 54, 57–58, 67, 96n8
U.S. Congress: Indian gaming laws, 56; list of acts, 60; tribal sovereignty laws, 45–47, 54–55
U.S. Constitution, 44
U.S. Supreme Court decisions, 44–45, 54–56

Vizenor, Erma, 91n30
Vizenor, Gerald, 80

Waadookodaading Ojibwe Immersion Charter School, 78
Wabamikee, Mark, 76
Wakonabo, Mark, 79
War of 1812, 16
Warren, William, 80
Wars: with British, 16; with Dakota, 20–23; impact on fur trade, 14–17; with Iroquois, 15–17; Wounded Knee Trading Post, 64, 95n5

Washington, DC, delegations to, 29
Water, Michael, 4
Weise, Jeffrey, 93n49
White Earth Indian Agency, 38
White Earth Land Settlement Act (1986), 37, 91n28
White Earth Ojibwe: enrolled membership, 71; land cessions and allotments, 35–37, 91n28
White Earth Reservation: casinos, effect of, 57; Indian Police Force, 41; removal and relocation to, 28–29; repatriated items, 53; traditional ceremonies, 24, 77–78, 80; tribal government, 43, 91n30, 92n31; U.S. government control of, 31
Wicoie Nandagikendan Early Childhood Immersion Project, 79
Wilbur, Sylvia, 83
Wild rice harvesting, 9, 10, 11, 76, 82–83
Wilkinson, Melville C., 39
Wind-Reyes, Jennifer, 62–63
Wolfe, Vincent, 49
Women, gender roles, 8
Worcester v. Georgia, 44
Wounded Knee Trading Post, 64, 95n5
Writers and authors, 80

Picture Credits

Map on page vi   Matthew D. Hill
Images on pages viii, 7, 61, 68, 77, 78, 82   courtesy the author
Image on page 15   WHi-1900, Wisconsin Historical Society
Image on page 39   WHi 29030, Wisconsin Historical Society
Image on page 44   from iStock.com
Images on page 49   by D. Kakkak, published in the *Circle,* May 1990
Image on page 50   courtesy Judy Olausen
Image on page 55   courtesy National Archives
Image on page 57   Bois Forte Band of Chippewa
Images on page 63   courtesy Dick Bancroft
Image on page 64   www.BillHackwell.com
Image on page 66   WHi 35070, Wisconsin Historical Society
Image on page 73   courtesy Joseph J. Allen
Image on page 76 top   courtesy Great Lakes Indian Fish and Wildlife Commission, Odanah, Wisconsin
Images on page 76 bottom   courtesy Janet Cardle

All others from MHS collections

Acknowledgments

Research for this book includes secondary, archival, and oral sources, involving numerous interviews with Ojibwe elders and Indian leaders. Their knowledge about tribal languages, cultures, and history is a very important contribution to this work. It simply would not have been possible without the assistance of Luella Seelye, Melvin Eagle, James Clark, Raining Boyd, Richard "Dick" Barber, David Aubid, Connie "Babe" Rivard, Dora Ammann, Archie Mosay, Betsy Schultz, Delorse Rogers, Joseph Auginaush, Susan Jackson, Hartley White, Walter "Porky" White, Emma Fisher, Collins Oakgrove, Mary Roberts, Edward Benton-Banai, Charles "Scott" Headbird, Anna Gibbs, Margaret Porter, Thomas Stillday, Eugene Stillday, Marlene Stately, Leona Wakonabo, Albert Churchill, Thomas Goldtooth, Daniel Jones, Dennis Jones, Nancy Jones, Vernon Whitefeather, Clyde Bellecourt, Sean Fahrlander, Ada Deer, and Earl Otchingwanigan (Nyholm). Thank you to Thomas Vennum, Jim Northrup, Jason Schlender, Wesley Ballinger, and Michael Swan for help with pictures. This book was also graced by the scrutiny and editorial advice of Gwenyth Swain, Shannon Pennefeather, David Thorstad, and David, Robert, and Margaret Treuer, all of whom made it better.

My research for this project was at times and in different ways supported financially by grants and fellowships from the Minnesota Humanities Center, the National

Endowment for the Humanities/National Science Foundation Documenting Endangered Languages Fellowship Program, the American Philosophical Society, the Bush Leadership Fellows Program, and the John Simon Guggenheim Foundation.

Any major research and writing endeavor takes tremendous commitments of time and energy. I received unbounded support and encouragement. For that, I have a great many people to thank, not the least of whom are friends Alfred Bush, Earl Otchingwanigan (Nyholm), John Nichols, Thomas Stillday, Anna Gibbs, Eugene Stillday, Archie Mosay, Dora Ammann, Brooke Ammann, Keller Paap, Lisa LaRonge, Rick and Penny Kagigebi, Isadore Toulouse, Daniel Jones, Dennis Jones, Sean Fahrlander, Dustin Burnette, Charles Grolla, Jeremy Kingsbury, Daniel York, Lahnah Rossbach, James Hardy, Diane Thompson, Adrian Liberty, Henry Flocken, Philip Deloria, Donald Fixico, Richard White, Michael Witgen, Bruce Fetter, Shalah Kingbird, Melissa Greene, Deborah Eagle, Thomas Saros, Brenda Child, Gitendra and Dilhani Uswatte, Vivasvan Soni, Ursula Swiney, Ab and Carol Boonswang, Brendan Weickert, Jamie and George "Skaff" Elias, Bryan Lee, Jean Higaki, Timothy Chow, Aditya Adarkar, Daniel Stevens, Bruce Godfrey, Andrew Tallon, Eric Lin, Aryani Ong, Arthur and Grace Mateos, Paul and Amy Johnson, Sumio Yamada, Scott Lyons, Diane Amour, Donna Beckstrom, David Thorstad, Donald Day, Paul Day, Kent Smith, Benjamin Burgess, Tori Dahlke, Joseph Aitken, Lee Cook, Robert Shimek, Thomas Goldtooth, Renee Gurneau, Audrey Thayer, Judy Fairbanks, Andrew and Mary Favorite, Michael and Patty Smith, Gene Youngdahl, Ted Waukey, Leon Valliere, Linda Wade, Irene Benjamin, Chad Uran, Michael Bowman, Susan Hallett, Skip and Babette Sandman, Leonard and Mary Moose, James and Betsy McDougall, Eunice Lighfeather, Earl Hoagland, Paul DeMain, Patrick Carriere, Michael Sullivan, Michael, Midge, Frank, and Mark Montano, and Nancy Erickson.

I am also always forever indebted to my greatest support base of all in my family—my parents Robert and Margaret Treuer, my siblings Smith, Paul, Derek, Megan, Micah, and David Treuer, their spouses, Gretchen Potter, Ronna, Mary, Debbie, and Elissa Treuer, my children Jordan, Robert, Madeline, Caleb, Isaac, Elias, Evan, and Mia, and my wife, Blair. Nothing would be possible without you.

Minnesotans can trace their families and their state's heritage to a multitude of ethnic groups. *The People of Minnesota* series tells each group's story in a compact, handsomely illustrated, and accessible paperback. Readers will learn about the group's accomplishments, ethnic organizations, settlement patterns, and occupations. Each book includes a personal story of one person or family, told through a diary, a letter, or an oral history.

Minnesota writer Bill Holm reminded us why these stories remain as important as ever: "To be ethnic, somehow, is to be human. Neither can we escape it, nor should we want to. You cannot interest yourself in the lives of your neighbors if you don't take sufficient interest in your own."

This series is based on the critically acclaimed book *They Chose Minnesota: A Survey of the State's Ethnic Groups* (Minnesota Historical Society Press). The volumes in *The People of Minnesota* bring each group's story up to date and add dozens of photographs to inform and enhance the telling.

Books in the series include *Irish in Minnesota, Jews in Minnesota, Norwegians in Minnesota, African Americans in Minnesota,* and *Germans in Minnesota.*

About the Author

Anton Treuer is professor of Ojibwe at Bemidji State University and editor of *Living Our Language: Ojibwe Tales and Oral Histories, Aaniin Ekidong: Ojibwe Vocabulary Project, Omaa Akiing,* and the *Oshkaabewis Native Journal,* the only academic journal of the Ojibwe language.